T'AI
CHI
CH'UAN
AND
I CHING

T'AI
CHI
CH'UAN
AND
I CHING

**A Choreography
of Body and Mind**

Da Liu

PERENNIAL LIBRARY

HARPER & ROW, PUBLISHERS, New York
Cambridge, Philadelphia, San Francisco
Washington, London, Mexico City
São Paulo, Singapore, Sydney

Acknowledgment is made for permission to reprint quotations from the following
copyrighted material:

THE I CHING: OR BOOK OF CHANGES, translated by Richard Wilhelm, rendered into
English by Cary F. Baynes, Bollingen Series XIX (copyright 1950 and © 1967 by
Bollingen Foundation). Reprinted by permission of Princeton University Press.

First PERENNIAL LIBRARY edition published 1987.

To order an instructional videotape containing the complete movements of T'ai Chi
Ch'uan found in this book send a check for $70.00 to the T'ai Chi Society of New
York, 520 West 110th Street, Apt. 7A, New York, NY 10025.

Library of Congress Catalog Card Number: 79-183640
ISBN: 0-06-091309-6

CONTENTS

V. THE TAO OF SELF-DEFENSE   74

VI. TAOIST MEDITATION AND T'AI CHI CH'UAN   85

VII. The *T'ai Chi Ch'uan Classics*   90

NOTES   121

PREFACE

The first edition of *T'ai Chi Ch'uan and I Ching,* published in 1972, sold out in three months and had to be reprinted. It has been through many printings over a decade and a half and has sold almost a million copies. It has been a very successful book and is certainly proof of the growing popularity of T'ai Chi Ch'uan in the West in recent years. I would like to take this opportunity to thank my readers for their enthusiasm.

I wrote three more books about the *I Ching:* in 1974, *I Ching Coin Prediction,* which was translated into German, Dutch, and Italian (a second edition was published in Great Britain by Routledge, Kegan Paul in 1984); *I Ching Numerology,* which came out in 1979; and *T'ai Chi Ch'uan and Meditation,* published by Schocken in 1986. I have also written three books related to Taoism: *The Tao of Health and Longevity, Tao and Chinese Culture,* published by Schocken, and the second edition of *Taoist Health Exercises,* published by Putnam in 1983. Thus the West has become steadily more informed about the relation of the *I Ching* to Chinese philosophy as a whole.

A few practitioners of T'ai Chi Ch'uan still express doubt that it is closely related to the *I Ching.* Although some books on T'ai Chi Ch'uan refer to the *I Ching,* they use the text marginally, without amalgamating it with T'ai Chi Ch'uan. To make the link between the *I Ching* and T'ai Chi Ch'uan clearer, I have added a new chapter on the waxing and waning of Ch'ien and K'un as applied to the practice of T'ai Chi Ch'uan. The phrase "T'ai Chi" itself originally comes from the *I Ching.* The concept has been widely used in Chinese culture, being found in areas as varied as medical science, meditation, and prediction, as well as in the exercise of T'ai Chi Ch'uan. I would like to give more information to the readers about the name and forms of the T'ai Chi Ch'uan. They all come from the T'ai Chi Tu, or Great Beginning. The fundamental elements of the T'ai Chi Ch'uan are the thirteen postures that were developed from the T'ai Chi Tu. (For details, see the last chapter of this book.) Whatever the discipline to which it is applied, the concept is rooted in the *I Ching*.

The *I Ching* is translated into English as *The Book of Changes,* but actually has three meanings: "ease," "change," and "changelessness." The basic principle of T'ai Chi Ch'uan is derived from all three. First is "ease," for the form should be comfortable and easy. Second is "change"; the form constantly changes from *yin* (heavy) to *yang* (light), never stopping. The exercise also involves mutual change: The weight always shifts from left to right or right to left. Even though there is this unceasing change, the body should still keep its balance and remain centered. The mind is always peaceful and relaxed. Thus the exercise embodies changelessness.

This edition also includes my translation of the *T'ai Chi Ch'uan Classics* and additional discussion about the Tao of self-defense. In my commentaries on the Classics, I use Taoist principles to clarify the spiritual and scientific connections to the T'ai Chi Ch'uan exercises. I am happy to be able to add the present work to the literature on this subject, and to have demonstrated the T'ai Chi Ch'uan form on videocassette and disk. These products are a helpful supplement to this book for the reader who desires to learn the form. They are available through bookstores and the T'ai Chi Society of New York.

I would like to thank the following for their help in completing this manuscript: Dr. John Lad, Jim Hickey, T. C. Chang, Reggie Jackson, Susan Delone, Kao Yu Ying Liu, Dr. Samuel Johnson, Rosemary Birardi, Paul Knopf, Sharon Wheeler Hadley, Steven Berko, Robert Clark, Noa Nothmann, Tracy Cochran, Duncan Cooper, Jorg Dreisorner-Lewis, and Jean Matthews.

July, 1986
New York

PREFACE TO
FIRST EDITION

I have been teaching T'ai Chi Ch'uan, a Chinese form of body movement, to students from all parts of the world for more than twenty years. Frequently I am asked questions about the practice of T'ai Chi Ch'uan: "Will it improve my physical condition?" "Can it relieve stress and tension?" "Will it put me 'in tune' with my body?" "In what ways is T'ai Chi Ch'uan related to Chinese thought?"

Many people who know even a little about T'ai Chi Ch'uan realize that it draws upon *yin* and *yang,* the passive and active principles of Chinese philosophy. They also know that the popular contemporary pastime of casting the *I Ching* is based on a world-view that utilizes the same concepts. Quite properly they have asked, "What is the relationship between T'ai Chi Ch'uan and the *I Ching?*" Such a connection exists in that each T'ai Chi movement is related to a particular hexagram of the *I Ching.* This relationship holds vital clues to a deeper understanding of Chinese thought which, like all valid world-views, is based on knowledge of the self gleaned from the practical experience of meditation. The movements of T'ai Chi Ch'uan and the hexagrams upon which they are based are both methods of describing the circulation of psychic energy in the body of the meditator.

This book is, to my knowledge, the first to explain in the English language the connection between the T'ai Chi movements and the hexagrams. I am well aware that in contemporary America the *I Ching* is regarded almost solely as a book of prediction. T'ai Chi Ch'uan is known in America as a physical exercise for relaxation and self-defense. While these views of T'ai Chi and the *I Ching* are not incorrect, they are very much like judging the value of a precious jewel by the opulent case in which it rests. The case may be attrac-

tive, arrayed in velvet and gold, but it is nothing in comparison to the
jewel buried securely inside.

T'ai Chi Ch'uan and the *I Ching* both allow one to discover that
most precious jewel, the nature of the Tao. They do this by revealing
the secrets of the Circulation of Light, the circulation of psychic
energy in meditation. T'ai Chi Ch'uan and the *I Ching* are the keys
by which the theoretical philosophy of Taoism can be converted to
a practical way of knowledge. Of course, even this kind of knowledge, if practiced without an experienced master and if practiced
under the wrong conditions, is not likely to lead anywhere.

I began my studies in 1928 in Kiang-su in East China under the
famous Sun Lu-tang, a master who founded the Sun School of T'ai
Chi Ch'uan. Later, I traveled to the Southwest Provinces where I met
and studied with great T'ai Chi masters. I then changed from the Sun
to the Yang School, the form which I teach today.

I hope that this book will enable the earnest seeker to realize the
depth and magic of both the *I Ching* and T'ai Chi Ch'uan. I also hope
that it will encourage the T'ai Chi student to greater proficiency and
inspiration in his practice.

Many people helped me in the preparation of this book. They have
my sincere appreciation: Herbert Cohen, Earl George, Joseph
Month, Barbara Rosenthal, Richard Shulman, Carol Southern, Olive
Wong, and James Wyckoff.

Da Liu

New York City
December 1971

T'AI
CHI
CH'UAN
AND
I CHING

I. INTRODUCTION

T'ai Chi Ch'uan Today

Although its roots are in ancient China, T'ai Chi Ch'uan is very suitable for tense Westerners. It has the advantages of regular exercise combined with a definite emphasis on the gracefulness and slowness of pace that Western society so conspicuously lacks. T'ai Chi Ch'uan can give those who live in industrialized fast-paced cities a compensating factor in their lives. It relaxes the mind as well as the body. It helps digestion, quiets the nervous system, benefits the heart and blood circulation, makes joints loose, and refreshes the skin.

Any age group can practice T'ai Chi. Liu Sho-ting, a contemporary T'ai Chi master, at eighty-four years of age still teaches it to students. He began to practice after he had a heart attack at the age of sixty. In three years, he was out of danger with a stronger and more vigorous body than before.

In the beginning one needs a large space to practice. More advanced students need only four square feet. The movements can be performed without any cumbersome equipment. Teamwork, although sometimes enjoyable, is unnecessary. Only for pushing hands, the T'ai Chi form of self-defense, are two people required. Appropriate in any season of the year and in any weather, like the Tao itself, T'ai Chi is unlimited in its benefits and the conditions in which it reveals its nature. It is best to practice the forms two times a day: in the morning when arising and before going to bed in the evening. During lunch, it can be done in the office. Throughout the world T'ai Chi is performed for a variety of reasons. Dance and theater schools in America use it as part of their training routines. Medical institutions in China use it to aid in restoring health. In New York it is even taught in old-age homes. For daily exercise and for maintaining health it is an ideal regimen.

Personally, I agree with the great master Chang San-feng when he said, "This exercise will lead many practitioners to health, happiness, and longevity. The defense is secondary." I don't like to emphasize competition or pushing hands in my classes. Still, in its proper place, T'ai Chi Ch'uan is an effective defense form and I teach it when I am sure sufficient forms have been mastered.

T'ai Chi can help both men and women enhance their personal appearance. Beauty is not confined to the face but penetrates the whole body. The relaxed, gentle movements of T'ai Chi Ch'uan keep the body from being tense and awkward. The forms also keep the body erect and well-postured. Since muscular tension drains the fine blood vessels of the face and hands from an adequate supply of blood, the relief provided by T'ai Chi corrects this condition, pouring color and life into neglected parts as water to a flower. Adequate oxygen and blood circulation prevent a person from appearing old.

There are many schools of T'ai Chi Ch'uan. The Yang School, which I follow, is derived from the Chen School. Four generations have continued the Yang School considerably beyond its predecessor. The Yang School has great influence in Chinese society and is also the most popular there and abroad. Another, the Wu School, was developed out of the Yang School in the 1920s. It is popular mostly in Hong Kong. One more, the Sun School, was created by Sun Lu-tang, a master of symbolical forms. But it is not too popular today. Sun is better known for his work in *Sheng I* and *Pa-Kua* (Eight Trigram) boxing.

The high forms, in which the body is kept upright, are best for the beginner and the old person. The more advanced student should use the low forms with their large steps and low-postured body, necessitating particularly loose joints and flexible limbs. The middle forms, neither high nor low, are suitable for the average student.

The long form of the Yang School has 108 different postures. It is like the Yangtze River, long but gently flowing. It lasts fifteen to twenty minutes when fully comprehended. The professional T'ai Chi student should learn this form. The short form, which is recommended for the average student, is much easier to learn, comprising about fifty forms and taking from seven to ten minutes or less to perform. It is good for the office worker and for people who wish to improve their health and can be practiced two or three times a day.

If you wish to learn T'ai Chi Ch'uan, you must first be positively determined in mind. In order to achieve proficiency daily practice is desirable. It must become an essential part of your life. Second, you should find a good teacher. He will give you a combination of correct forms and the deep philosophy underlying it. He will inspire you to achieve the strong yet subtle concentration necessary to master these forms.

The Origin of T'ai Chi Ch'uan

Before pursuing the shadowy history of T'ai Chi Ch'uan, it is well to note that the hexagrams, the *I Ching,* the concept of *yin-yang,* and the sophisticated methods and philosophy of Taoist meditation preceded it. While the inspiration for T'ai Chi may very well have come from nature—from the observation of animals, for instance— its actual source of energy lies entirely within.

Many credit Chang San-feng of the Sung Dynasty (960–1278) with the development of T'ai Chi Ch'uan in the twelfth century. Others say that he lived in the thirteenth or even in the sixteenth century. He is said to have had two important predecessors, an Indian monk named Ta Mo, who came to China to practice meditation, and a wood-cutter named Hsü Hsuan-ping, who lived a century and a half after Ta Mo (around 750). Ta Mo supposedly invented his *Shiao-lin* exercise, a series of movements similar to some of the T'ai Chi movements, for the physically degenerated monks of the Shiao-lin Monastery. He wished to strengthen their bodies so that they could be a more secure temple for the soul. Hsü Hsuan-ping performed the Long Boxing Exercise, a series of movements which contain many forms of contemporary T'ai Chi, such as Single Whip, White Crane Spreads Wings, and Step Forward, Seven Stars.

But legend has it that the firmest and most complete foundations of the T'ai Chi Ch'uan came from the famous Taoist Chang San-feng, known as the Immortal. He is said to have been an ardent follower of Confucius and to have had a strong interest in the *I Ching.* He had a prominent position as a magistrate in the Chung-san district in China. Later he gave up his official capacities to become a hermit. Still alive in the Ming Dynasty, he continued to study under various

enlightened Taoists. Traveling from place to place, he learned techniques of meditation and the martial arts.

According to the legendary story, Chang San-feng, in the house
meditating at noon, heard an unusual noise in the courtyard. Looking
down from his window, he saw a snake with raised head, hissing in
challenge to a crane in the tree above. The crane flew down from
the pine tree and attacked the snake with its swordlike beak. But the
snake turned its head aside and attacked the crane's neck with its tail.
The crane used its right wing to protect its neck. Then the snake
darted against the crane's legs. The crane raised its left leg and
lowered its left wing to combat the assailant. Stabbing again and
again, the bird was unable to make a solid blow. The snake, twisting
and bending, was always out of reach. After a while, tired of fighting,
the crane flew back to the tree and the snake slithered into the hole
in the tree trunk. There they rested in preparation for their encounter
the following day.

Chang San-feng watched this performance from his window
again and again. From it he realized the value of yielding in the
face of strength. In the combat of the crane and the snake, he
saw in living form the principle of the *I Ching:* the strong changing to the yielding and the yielding changing to the strong. He
remembered the teaching: "What is more yielding than water?
Yet back it comes to wear down the stone." The great master
studied the crane and the snake, the wild animals, the clouds, the
water and the trees bending in the wind. He codified these natural movements into a system of exercise. From the action of the
crane came the form White Crane Spreads Wings. From the action of the snake came Snake Creeps Down. The crane attacking
with his beak gave Brush Knee and Push. Constructing other
forms based on the movements he had seen, he also adapted
Shiao-lin martial sets to the idea of Taoist meditation.

Chang San-feng taught his disciples Taoism and meditation in the
White Clouded Temple in Peking West Mountain. He created another school for T'ai Chi and other exercises in Hu-pei Province on
the Wu-tang Mountain. This was known as the Wu-tang School and
stood in contrast to the Shiao-lin School for several hundred years.
We owe the present forms of T'ai Chi to numerous masters who
utilized and perfected their techniques over many centuries.

The *I Ching*

The *I Ching* is one of the first efforts of the human mind to place itself in the universe. A collection and interpretation of a series of sixty-four 6-line figures called hexagrams, it has exerted a living influence in China for three thousand years. The individual hexagrams predate the *Book of Changes*. They were preserved on wood tablets long before they were recorded by King Wen in 1150 B.C.

The *I Ching* eventually became the most important of the Five Confucian Classics *(History, Odes, Ritual, Spring and Autumn,* and *Change)* and was the only one of these spared when Emperor Ch'in Shih Huang Ti ordered all the ancient books burned in 213 B.C. Its antiquity and worth is substantiated by its use as a common source for both Confucian and Taoist philosophies for many centuries.

The Chinese character for *I* in *I Ching* signifies both change and changelessness. It is constructed from the characters that make up those of the sun and moon, which, although appearing and disappearing each day and night, remain a changeless feature of the heavens. *I* also denotes easiness and clarity. These meanings suggest the clarity with which nature, society, and the individual are revealed through the agency of the sixty-four hexagrams. *Ching* means a book or classic written by a sage.

Each of the hexagrams consists of two 3-lined figures called trigrams. There are eight basic trigrams constructed from a combination of unbroken and broken lines. The trigrams, like the mathematical symbols x and y, can stand for many things. For instance, the trigram *Ch'ien* can mean heaven (the natural world), leader or king (the social realm), father (family relationship), head (part of body), strength (quality), and other things as well. Combined in a hexagram, the symbols acquire a distinct composite meaning. Each line shows a different aspect of the situation pictured by the hexagram.

The creation of the eight trigrams is attributed to Fu Shi, the legendary Chinese sage who reputedly lived during the age of hunting and fishing around 5,000 years ago. By studying and observing heaven, earth, animal tracks, and his own body, he devised the broken and unbroken line as symbols of the fundamental nature of the universe. From these, he constructed eight trigrams, each of which stood for an aspect of nature, society, and the individual.

The origin of the sixty-four hexagrams is unclear. Supposedly, they were created after the time of Fu Shi. King Wen composed his book during his captivity, following his arrest by Emperor Shing Chu. He spent seven years in prison, studying the hexagrams by night and day. He structured his findings in the form of predictions which implied other meanings besides divination. King Wen's codification led to a commentary consisting of the Judgment, the Image, and the text attached to individual lines of the hexagrams. His son, the Duke of Chou, completed the work by adding to the text a commentary known as the Decision, which clarifies the Judgment of the hexagram and discusses the philosophy out of which the prediction develops.

The last contribution to the *I Ching* was made by the great Chinese philosopher Confucius, who, with his students, wrote a complete and detailed treatise on the philosophy of the book as it then existed. This section is called the Ten Wings. The Ten Wings, which are like a book review, explain and analyze the history, philosophy, and spiritual meaning of the book. They include a detailed discussion of the trigrams (Eighth Wing, or chapter), a commentary on the Images (Third and Fourth Wings), and miscellaneous notes on the hexagrams (Tenth Wing).

Thus, the *I Ching* through the centuries evolved from simple unbroken and broken lines into a complete philosophical book.

The first English translation of the *I Ching* was made in the nineteenth century by James Legge, a Scottish missionary and scholar. Since that time, more than twenty English-language editions have been published. The best-known English version of the *I Ching* was first translated into German earlier in this century by Richard Wilhelm. Rendered into English by Cary F. Baynes, with an introduction by the distinguished psychiatrist Carl G. Jung, this version, from which we shall often cite text, is arranged in three books: Book I consists of the sixty-four hexagrams and the Judgment, Images, and text for each line written by King Wen. Book II contains the Ten Wings written by Confucius, his students, and his disciples. Book III, the most useful in prediction, is made up of the hexagrams with the commentaries of both Confucius and the Duke of Chou. The commentaries discuss the meaning and symbolism of each hexagram.

The *I Ching* also gives practical advice on matters not directly connected with divination or philosophy. It includes information on government, numerology, astrology, cosmology, meditation, and military strategy. John Blofield, in his version of the *I Ching,* says that is was used regularly by generals of the Japanese army during the Russo-Japanese War in 1904–1905. Although its wisdom took root in China, the *I Ching* is an integral part of the cultural heritage of Japan, Korea, Vietnam, and other Far Eastern countries. Its impact on the West is just beginning. At this moment the hexagrams are being developed for computer use, and in this form their wisdom will be available to the uninitiated on an entirely different level.

> The Changes is a book
> From which one may not hold aloof.
> Its tao is forever changing—
> Alteration, movement without rest,
> Flowing through the six empty places;
> Rising and sinking without fixed law,
> Firm and yielding transform each other.
> They cannot be confined within a rule;
> It is only change that is at work here. . . .
>
> They also show care and sorrow and their causes.
> Though you have no teacher,
> Approach them as you would your parents.[1]

Yin-Yang and Taoism

The concept of *yin-yang* is often associated with the name of Lao-tzu. Actually it was discovered and used for something like 4,800 years, several thousand years before Lao-tzu and his famous work, the *Tao Teh Ching,* which enunciated the principles of Taoism. The polarities of *yin* and *yang* exist everywhere, in everything and in every time. In the *I Ching* and Taoist thought heaven is *yang,* earth is *yin;* sun is *yang,* moon is *yin;* man is *yang,* woman is *yin;* firmness is *yang,* yielding is *yin.* In the body, the head is *yang* and the belly is *yin.* Since this duality penetrates all of nature we can, of course, find many other examples.

In T'ai Chi Ch'uan the light foot is *yang* and the heavy, firmly placed foot, *yin*. The light forms are *yang;* the heavy are *yin*. A *yang* form will always follow a *yin* form, one going forward or to one side, the other going back.

Lao-tzu, although not the inventor of this concept, expounded it magnificently. He lived between 604 and 531 B.C., though legend has it that he lived to be several hundred years old. In his youth he was supposedly a librarian who kept documents in the time of the Chu Dynasty. But he gave up his job and went to live alone as a hermit in far West China. He is said to have been the Immortal who passed on to Buddha the secret of immortality. Legend also has it that he met Confucius and awed him by his superior wisdom. Whatever the validity of these stories, Lao-tzu expounded the philosophy of the Tao most eloquently.

The spirit of Taoism demands a vigorous and wholehearted devotion to Truth and a rather secondary interest in secular affairs if they conflict with devotion. Perhaps this is why many Taoist masters have been accused of laziness and unwillingness to assume responsibilities. One such story illustrating the Taoist attitude toward the world is told about the great master Chuang-tzu, whose writings concerning Taoism are said to be more precise and complete than those of his predecessor, Lao-tzu. He lived around 370 to 300 B.C.

It seems that one day Chuang-tzu was fishing in the Pu River when two civil servants arrived to speak to him. They came with a message from the King of Ch'u: "I wish to trouble you by putting you in charge of everything within my territories."

But Chuang-tzu did not drop his fishing rod. Without looking at the officials, he said, "I hear that in Ch'u there is a sacred tortoise shell whose wearer, the tortoise, died three thousand years ago. And I hear the king who sent you keeps this shell in his ancestral temple in a sacred hamper covered with a sacred cloth. Was it better for the tortoise to die and to leave its shell to be honored? Or would it have been better for that tortoise to live and keep on dragging its tail through the mud?" (In China, tortoises are said to live forever.)

The two officials responded, "Why, it would have been better for it to live and to continue to draw its sacred tail after it over the mud."

"Go your ways," said the sage, matter-of-factly. "I will continue to drag my tail after me through the mud."

Despite this attitude, Taoism did, in fact, intrude its influence into Chinese civil affairs. At the same time the great Taoist master Wang Chen taught, two Taoist strategists, Sun-pin from the state of Chi and Pong-chuen, a general from the state of Wei, became enmeshed in a military struggle against each other. At the end Sun-pin killed Pong-chuen, and Taoism was projected for the first time into a political and military struggle.

Although prayer, rituals, and magical spells have been associated with Taoist practice, as well as traditions of politics and military strategy, the real contribution of Taoism has been to the inner life of man. Its various schools of nonbeing, nonaction, inner and outer elixir have all pointed to the fact that before man can understand the world, he must understand himself. A key part of Taoist practice, therefore, has been the act of meditation. In meditation one learns to focus and direct energies which are usually squandered in the mundane perceptions of the five senses. In Taoist meditation these energies are directed through two main channels: *Tu Mu,* a channel along the spinal column from the base of the spine, where a psychic center called *wei lu* is located, to a psychic center at the top of the head called *ni wan* and over the head to the upper lip; and *Jen Mu,* a channel which passes down the front of the body to the genital region *(huei yin).*

Taoist teaching utilizes both T'ai Chi Ch'uan and the hexagrams to demonstrate the flow of psychic energy *(chi)* along these two channels. The movements of the *chi* are called the Greater and the Lesser Heavenly Circulation. The movements of the arms and legs in T'ai Chi Ch'uan, along with the turns and posturing of the body, help to picture the flow of *chi* during meditation. Also, the very structure of the hexagrams can be used to picture the human body, the two top lines being the head, the middle lines being the chest, and the bottom two being the lower part of the body. The *I Ching* itself can be read as a manual describing the course of the *chi* in meditation and as a guide to the temptations and goals of the meditator.

II. THE PRINCIPLES OF MOVEMENT IN T'AI CHI CH'UAN

The movements of T'ai Chi Ch'uan are based on the coordination of the mind, the inner body, and the outer body.

Mind

It is essential for the mind of the student to be still and concentrated. If the mind is not resolute, the forms will not be achieved. The right mental attitude for practicing is concentrated quietness. This is also the attitude of meditation, in which the outside moves inside. But in T'ai Chi Ch'uan the opposite occurs: the inside moves outside.

Inner Movement

BREATHING

Buddhists refer to breathing as the wheel of law which turns uniformly and unceasingly. Breath is the energy of life. Without breath, there is no life. Taoists regard it as one of the three treasures of the body. The T'ai Chi practitioner regulates his breathing in harmony with the movement of his body to achieve health and the coordination required for self-defense.

Breathing is not only a matter of inhalation and exhalation. It also involves the circulation of the inner vital force called *chi*. When mind, breath, and sexual energy are brought together, *chi* is produced. In order to accomplish deep inner breathing, one must concentrate the *chi* into a psychic center known as the *tan tien*, located three inches below the navel. The *tan tien* may be compared to the boiler of a steam engine. When the mind concentrates there, heat is developed. The excess energy, like the excess water evaporated in the boiler, is then distributed to the rest of the body, propelling the limbs of the T'ai Chi player.

This process of concentration and circulation of *chi,* in turn, produces another substance which we may call spirit, or in Taoist terminology, *shen.* The conversion of one inner essence into another can be likened to an alchemical process. Sexual energy, often referred to literally in the Taoist texts as sperm, is converted into *chi* by mind concentration. Then *chi* is refined to become spirit (or *shen*). The *shen* is further refined to become emptiness *(shu).* In this manner the inner vital force is changed from one state to another, just as the matter of common experience goes through various phases from solid to liquid to gas. According to legend, the master who has reached emptiness has developed an indestructible body and has achieved immortality.

BLOOD CIRCULATION

Like breathing the circulation of the blood is essential to life. The breath controls the circulation of the blood. The T'ai Chi Ch'uan student uses movement to help the *chi,* the inner energy, accelerate the circulation of the blood. Blood circulation and *chi* together propel the limbs in much the same way that gas or steam sets a machine in motion.

Outer Movement

The outer movements of the forms of T'ai Chi Ch'uan are based on principles which are an integral part of the T'ai Chi art.

SMOOTHNESS

Movement should be smooth and even. The student executes all the forms at the same tempo. No movement is sudden or abrupt.

From beginning to end the body moves with the same smooth dynamics.

BALANCE

Each form requires balance. The practitioner leans neither forward nor backward, neither to the right nor to the left. If he loses his balance the player will get into difficulty, feeling uncomfortable and perhaps even falling.

CENTERING

The torso of the body should be erect and in a central position. In the back, from the coccyx to the crown of the head, the body of the student should be a straight line. In the front from the crown of the head to the chest and down to the lower abdomen there should also be a straight line. When the body is erect every bone and inner organ is in its proper position.

In using T'ai Chi for self-defense, the player's body is like a bow and arrow which goes directly to its goal. With practice he learns to achieve this accuracy automatically, without having to look or consciously aim his blows. He can apportion his strength correctly because he himself is centered.

Not only the torso, but the lower body must also be centered. The legs and feet are positioned so that they can pivot freely as well as carry heavy weight without injury. The weight should be placed in the middle of the feet, neither on the toes nor on the heels. In this way the practitioner can support his whole body without fatigue.

RELAXATION

Relaxation of the body and mind is crucial today because of the pace of our industrial cities. The ability to relax is a natural human instinct and, when developed, can aid in the prevention of disease. Both physical and mental relaxation are necessary in order to achieve mastery of the art of T'ai Chi Ch'uan. When the whole body is relaxed, the breath can go directly to the abdomen. The oxygen mixed with the blood can then penetrate into the muscles, just as water penetrates soil. The player should relax his thighs and waist so that he can move freely and without tension. When the legs are relaxed, the body is stable and can move very lightly.

CONTINUITY

In the *Book of Changes* every hexagram develops out of the one before it. Likewise in T'ai Chi Ch'uan, each form follows uninterruptedly and naturally from the previous one. In Chinese thought T'ai Chi Ch'uan is compared to a long river that flows freely and peacefully. It is recorded that Confucius, standing by a river, remarked that everything flows on and on like a river.

COORDINATION

Coordination of body, mind, and breathing is essential. The mind directs the breathing which should parallel the direction of the form. When the form is open or forward, the student inhales. When the form is closed or in retreat, he exhales. This movement of the breath allows the lungs to act as a bellows which pushes the stagnant air out and lets the fresh air in. The arms must be coordinated with the legs and the head with the torso so that none of the parts moves at a faster or slower pace than the others.

How to Practice

The student should let the following points guide him in order to achieve perfection of form:

SLOWNESS

T'ai Chi Ch'uan should be performed slowly and carefully so that the utmost quiet will be achieved. When food is chewed slowly, the taste of it can be fully realized and its digestion can supply more nourishment to the body. In the same way the T'ai Chi player moves slowly through the forms to enhance his concentration, energy, breath control, and patience.

HEAVINESS AND LIGHTNESS

The distribution of weight on the feet is constantly shifted. Sometimes the full weight of the body is on one foot while the other foot is completely light. The same principle is followed in the *I Ching* with regard to the changing lines of the hexagrams. A line with the value nine is completely light, while a six is absolute weight. When a six or a nine is received in divination, it means that the line will change to its opposite (broken to unbroken, unbroken to broken) and a new hexagram will be formed. Sometimes the weight in the T'ai Chi forms is 80 percent on one foot and 20 percent on the other. Sometimes it is 70 percent on one and 30 percent on the other. It is constantly changing. Only at the beginning and at the end is the weight placed equally on both feet.

EFFORTLESSNESS

Because ordinary exercises use strength, the result is often tension and fatigue. T'ai Chi Ch'uan, however, is based on effortlessness. Its movements are free and smooth. All unnecessary exertion is avoided. Less strength is used to produce more strength, as with a lever used to move heavy bodies. Moving smoothly and gracefully, without effort, the student achieves his art as naturally as a child in playing.

III. THE FORMS

T'ai Chi Ch'uan was originally divided into three sections, corresponding to the three primal powers—heaven, earth, and man—into
which each hexagram of the *I Ching* is divided. Here, however, I
have arranged the T'ai Chi movements in two sections. The first
section, containing few forms, is light like heaven. The second section, which has more forms, combines earth and man—the two
primal powers that stand under heaven.

The forms in the first section are executed toward the south
(Ch'ien), north *(K'un)*, west *(K'an)*, and east *(Li)*. These four trigrams
are components of the thirty hexagrams which make up Part I of the
Book of Changes. The forms in the first section are executed either
forward or backward, to the left or to the right.

In the second section there are not only more forms, but they are
executed closer to the ground and contain more kicks. From Bring
Tiger to the Mountain through Fair Lady Works at Shuttles the forms
are executed on the diagonal—toward the northeast *(Chen)*, southwest *(Sun)*, southeast *(Tui)*, and northwest *(K'en)*. These four trigrams are part of the hexagrams which make up Part II of the *Book
of Changes.*

In this book I have grouped the movements according to series.
The forms in each series are related to each other in meaning. I have
found that this arrangement makes it easier for the student to learn
and retain each form.

Part One

First Series

1. BEGINNING OF THE T'AI CHI CH'UAN

Stand erect, hands easily at sides, palms back. Heels are together, toes slightly apart (Fig. 1).

Sinking slightly with soft knees, shift weight onto right foot and step with left foot, toes straight forward, to the side so that feet are shoulder-width apart. Shift weight to left, and pivot on right heel to move right toes straight forward. Distribute weight evenly on both feet.

Let arms rise upward to shoulder height in front; draw wrists toward shoulders, fingers slightly straightening (Fig. 2).

Continue the circular movement, gently pressing hands down to sides again. The body rises slightly with the arms and sinks again as arms return to sides.

2. GRASP BIRD'S TAIL *(left)*

The left hand reaches up, palm inward, to hold the bird's neck; the right hand moves down as though smoothing the long plumage of the bird's tail.

Shift weight to left leg; pivoting on right heel, turn to right. Simultaneously the right arm rises, elbow bent, with hand at shoulder height; the left arm rises and crosses body at waist level, palm up. The palms are approximately toward each other (Fig. 3).

Shift weight forward onto right foot and pivot on left toes to turn slightly to the left. Step left with left foot, straight forward and a little left. Simultaneously the weight shifts forward on left foot, the left hand moves up to chin level, palm facing in; the right arm returns to right side, and as the body turns to left the right toes move slightly inward (Fig. 4).

Fig. 1

Fig. 2

Fig. 3

Fig. 4

Second Series

3. PUSH UP

Moving most of weight to left leg, the right foot pivots on toes as the body turns right.

Step with right foot slightly forward and a little right, heel first, toes straight ahead. Moving weight forward to right leg, left toes turn in as the right hand curves up and directly ahead to chin level with palm facing in, and left palm touches right palm (Fig. 5).

4. PULL BACK

Turn both hands over so left palm faces up toward right palm and right palm faces down, at the same time moving hands together diagonally to the right and up.

With weight shifting back to left leg, the hands fall down across body to left, the waist moving slightly left (Fig. 6).

5. PRESS FORWARD

The left forearm circles back, palm forward, and returns, pressing forward past left ear to right palm which simultaneously circles up on left side, palm in (Fig. 7). The palms move to the front of the body, the weight shifts to the right leg and pushes the arms forward.

6. PUSH FORWARD

Separate hands to shoulder width. The weight shifts back to the left leg and draws the arms in toward body at shoulder height. The weight moves forward to right leg and arms move forward (Fig. 8).

7. SINGLE WHIP

In this movement the left hand resembles a single whip.

The weight shifts to left leg, which slightly straightens arms, while the right toes are lifted.

Fig. 5

Fig. 6

Fig. 7

Fig. 8

Pivoting on the right heel, turn body 135 degrees, arms still extended and moving with the body.

Shift weight to right foot and pivot on left toes, turning body to face left. Simultaneously left arm moves across body at waist, palm up; right arm extends to right side of body, fingers pinched, hand at shoulder height. The elbow points to the floor (Fig. 9).

With weight on right leg, pivot on left toes to turn left, facing forward, opening arms to front.

Left foot takes a wide step forward and to the left. The weight moves to the left foot, the left hand turns palm over as it moves up to press forward with fingertips at throat height as the right toes move inward, pivoting on heel (Fig. 10).

Third Series

8. PLAY GUITAR *(right)*

With most of weight on left leg, turn right, pivoting on right toes. Arms remain at same height and open at the sides, palms facing forward. Move right leg left onto its heel, keeping the toes straight forward. Simultaneously the palms and arms close in, the left palm facing the right elbow at a five-inch distance (Fig. 11).

9. PULL BACK

Keeping the weight on left leg, draw the right foot back on its toes and close to the left foot, dropping hands toward and alongside the left leg, palms facing leg (Fig. 12).

10. STEP FORWARD AND STRIKE WITH SHOULDER

Step forward with right foot, toes straight, shifting weight to right foot and press body forward to the right side. Simultaneously the left hand moves across the right to lightly touch right wrist (Fig. 13).

Fig. 9

Fig. 10

Fig. 11

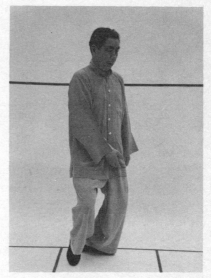

Fig. 12

11. White Crane Spreads Wings

Executing this form the T'ai Chi Ch'uan player resembles a crane standing with one foot delicately raised. The right hand is held in front of the forehead while the left remains at the side, indicating the crane's wings. The left foot is raised lightly, resembling the bird's foot.

With weight on right leg, move left leg in toward the right on toes, foot straight ahead and close to right foot. Simultaneously, the left hand moves to the left side, palm back, and the right hand moves up to the right side of the forehead, palm almost forward (Fig. 14).

Fourth Series

12. Brush Knee and Push *(left)*

Sinking slightly on right knee, turn slightly right as right arm lowers, palm up, and left arm moves up and across body to right side, palm down. Step left foot to the left front (Fig. 15).

The left arm continues around and downward to the left to brush across left knee and return to the left thigh.

The right hand comes down from behind the ear, elbow pointed downward, weight is shifted to the left leg as the right hand pushes forward (Fig. 16).

13. Play Guitar *(left)*

The right foot takes a small step by moving slightly in to the left, and weight shifts to right leg. The left foot moves in toward the right and in front onto its heel, and the arms move in reverse of Play Guitar *(right)*. The left foot and left hand extend farther than the right hand and foot (Fig. 17).

Fig. 13

Fig. 14

Fig. 15

Fig. 16

Fig. 17

14. Brush Knee and Push *(left)*

Circle arms around on right side and brush knee and push forward, as in Form 12, stepping left and forward with left foot and shifting weight to the left leg.

15. Step Forward and Punch

Shifting weight to the right, lower the right hand to groin, palm toward body, as left toes turn slightly outward. The right arm bends at elbow and lifts to chest height, making a fist (Fig. 18). Step onto left leg with toes straight ahead as left arm moves across waist level. As weight moves forward onto left leg, right-fisted arm moves forward, pushing through straight ahead (Fig. 19).

Fig. 18   Fig. 19

16. Draw Back and Push Forward

The left hand moves under right elbow and then pushes outward with back of hand. The right arm curves to the left and back as the fist opens.

Shifting the weight to the right leg, hands are drawn back (Fig. 20). Press forward, arms separating at shoulder height and width, palms down, as weight shifts to left leg.

17. Cross Hands

Shift weight to right foot, turn left toes inward, and open hands wide over head. Continue the arms down and forward and then up to cross at the wrists, chest level, palms in. The right foot pivots on toes and steps back to original straight-forward position (Fig. 21). To conclude Part One, repeat Form 1.

Fig. 20

Fig. 21

Part Two

First Series

18. BRING TIGER TO THE MOUNTAIN

Executing this form the player seems to hold the tiger as he steps forward. Tigers are popularly used in T'ai Chi forms owing to the legends of the friendly relationship between the gentle Taoist hermits and the animals of the forest. The tiger, when tamed, could be ridden on mountainous terrain as well as on the flatlands. It could even leap from cliff to cliff, with the masterful Taoist saint riding aloft with perfect tranquillity.

Shift weight to the left leg, make three-quarter turn diagonally to the right and step with right foot. Simultaneously the right arm drops, brushes across right knee with palm facing knee, the palm turning upward on the right side of the knee. The left arm drops back and curves upward to pass the ear as the fingertips press forward and seem to form a ball with right hand. As the arms move the weight shifts to the right, the left foot pivoting on heel (Fig. 22).

After completing Bring Tiger to the Mountain, repeat Forms 4, 5, 6, and 7, performing them on the diagonal rather than straight forward or to the side.

Second Series

19. FIST UNDER THE ELBOW

Shift weight to the right leg. The left foot steps left and forward as left arm swings to left, the palm down. The right foot takes a half-step forward and the right arm swings forward with it, the left arm curving down to the side (Fig. 22 a). Putting weight on right leg, the left heel is brought forward to face straight ahead (Fig. 22 b) with the left

Fig. 22

Fig. 22 a

Fig. 22 b

Fig. 23

Fig. 24

Fig. 25

arm moving with it, bending at the elbow; the right hand forms a fist which moves under the elbow (Fig. 23).

20. STEP BACK AND REPULSE MONKEY

The left hand grabs the monkey's hand as the right hand pushes the monkey's head away. At the same time, the player steps back.

From preceding form drop right arm to side. Turn left palm to face down and press fingertips forward.

As the body turns to the right, the right arm circles back, and both palms turn up (Fig. 24).

As the body turns forward, the right arm circles around and moves forward past the ear, the left arm falls to the side with the left foot stepping straight back. The right arm moves in front, fingertips pressing forward; the right toes straighten (Fig. 25). The left arm continues back as the body turns to the left.

Repeat these actions on the left side, and then again to the right.

21. SLANT FLYING

The hands sweep upward and downward in a diagonal motion, resembling the flying pattern of a bird winging low over the banks of a river.

Drop right hand across to left thigh (Fig. 26), cross left arm over the right hand. With the right foot take a large step to right and forward on the diagonal (135-degree angle), turning with the body.

The right arm moves diagonally up across the front of the body, palm slanting up. Simultaneously the left toes turn in and the left hand drops to the side (Fig. 27).

After completing Slant Flying, repeat Forms 8, 9, 10, 11, and 12.

Third Series

22. NEEDLE AT SEA BOTTOM

The player brings his hands downward to the sea of breath, the area below the navel. His right hand is held naturally straight, resem-

Fig. 26

Fig. 27

Fig. 28

Fig. 29

bling a needle, as he lowers both hands to knee height—to the bottom of the sea.

Take a small adjustment step to the left with right foot and shift weight to the right, placing left foot on its toes about eight inches in front of right foot. Lower and relax body and let palms drop down to knees, placing the left hand over the right wrist (Fig. 28).

23. PLAY ARMS LIKE A FAN

The hands are spread apart like the two sides of a Chinese folding fan.

Lift body, step forward and to the side with the left foot. Bring the right arm up, palm diagonally sideways to the right. The left arm moves in a forward arc, while the body turns slightly right simultaneously with these arm movements (Fig. 29).

24. TURN BODY AND STRIKE FIST TO BACK

Shift weight to the right and pivot on left heel to turn right. Simultaneously the right forearm moves straight out to the side and makes a fist, while the left arm drops to the side (Fig. 30).

Fourth Series

25. STEP FORWARD AND PUNCH

Turn right toes outward, step forward with left foot, and punch with right fist (Fig. 31). Then shift weight to right, step back with left foot, and pull hands back to left side.

26. HIT TIGER *(left, then right)*

One hand hits the tiger's forehead; another hits his chest.

The left palm turns up, and the right arm circles out, up and over, palm down. The arms then move diagonally across body to left as the left foot steps back (Fig. 32).

The arms continue to circle up and around in front to the right with

Fig. 30

Fig. 31

Fig. 32

Fig. 33

the right toes pivoting out. Shifting weight to the right, as arms continue to circle, step forward with the left foot; the arms move inward, making fists, to either side of the central body line, 11:30 o'clock with the left fist and 5:30 o'clock with the right fist, knuckles forward (Fig. 33).

Repeat the circular arm movements in reverse and continue as before but this time to the right.

27. Kick with Toes

The arms continue to circle up centrally, then out to the sides with palms forward. Here the right leg is lifted, and the toes kick forward and upward (Fig. 34).

The foot relaxes back in lifted position. Both hands move inward, form fists (Fig. 35), and brush down on either side of bent knee.

Fig. 34 Fig. 35

28. HIT OPPONENT'S EARS WITH FISTS

Step forward with right foot, moving weight onto right leg. The arms continue down, out, up, and around toward center to hit the imagined opponent's two ears (Fig. 36).

Fifth Series

29. TURN BODY AND KICK

Shift weight to the left leg, pivot on right heel to turn toes to the left; simultaneously drop hands (fists released) in an outward arc that circles up to come to rest at chest level, wrists crossed (Fig. 37).

Turn the right toes inward. Turn body to the left side and kick with left foot; the right hand moves up to protect the right temple with palm slightly forward, the left palm is forward and slightly down in the front (Fig. 38).

Fig. 36   Fig. 37

Fig. 38

30. Brush Knee and Push *(left)*

Repeat the movement described for Form 12.

31. Wave Hands Like a Cloud

The circular movements of the hands resemble the flowing motions of a cloud passing by in the sky.

With weight on left leg, pivot on right heel and turn to right. Shift weight to right leg and pivot on left heel to continue turn. Simultaneously the left hand moves across the front of the lower trunk, palm up, and the right hand is drawn back with the body in turning (Fig. 39). Left foot then steps forward, in line with and parallel to right foot. The width between the feet is slightly broader than shoulder width.

The body turns left from the waist as the weight moves to the left. Simultaneously the arms exchange: the right arm moves down across the lower trunk, palm up, and the left arm moves up and across to the left as the body turns (Fig. 40).

Alternating from right to left, this movement is repeated three, five, or seven times.

32. Single Whip

Repeat the movement described for Form 7.

Sixth Series

33. Snake Creeps Down

The hand moves down to the foot as the whole body sinks near to the ground. The motion is flowing and serpentine.

Pivot on right heel and turn right toes to the right side. Shift weight to right leg.

Pivot on left heel to turn toes inward while lowering body to sit almost on right heel. The right arm remains in Single Whip position but straightens. The left arm moves down along the inside of the lower thigh continuing down to pass the calf (Fig. 41).

Fig. 39

Fig. 40

Fig. 41

Fig. 42

Fig. 43

34. GOLDEN COCK ON ONE LEG *(left, then right)*

One hand is held down, the other held up. At the same time, the pose is frozen with one leg held up like a standing cock.

As the left arm continues to move forward across left calf, beginning upward sweep, the left toes turn forward again and the weight shifts to the left leg. The body lifts, the left hand moving up to strike, the right heel pivoting as the toes turn inward. The right arm lowers to the right side (Fig. 42).

The right arm and leg move together as the right arm moves up in an acute angle, palm to the side, and the right knee rises to strike forward, forming a right angle. Simultaneously the left arm drops to the left side (Fig. 43).

Repeat the movement, this time standing on right leg. Arms exchange movements and the left arm and knee move up together (Fig. 44).

Fig. 44

Fig. 45

35. HIGH PAT ON HORSE *(right)*

In this form the right hand sweeps upward to pat the horse's back as the left hand holds the reins.

Step back onto left foot, lowering left arm to waist level, palm up. The right hand moves up, palm down, across the left palm, as the weight begins to shift forward. As the weight moves forward onto the right leg, the body and hands move diagonally to the right, the hands also moving upward (right hand at forehead height; left hand above waist height) (Fig. 45).

36. SEPARATE FEET AND KICK *(right)*

As the weight shifts back onto left leg, the hands drop back and down to the left. Then left arm moves around the left side and to the front of the face, palm open, as right arm moves up to cross wrist with the left arm, palm open. As palms cross, the right foot moves onto its toes (Fig. 46).

The right toes kick low to the right diagonal while the arms slide

Fig. 46   Fig. 47

sideways, left hand at temple with palm forward, and right forearm moving from elbow to the right (Fig. 47).

37. HIGH PAT ON HORSE, AND SEPARATE FEET AND KICK *(left)*

Reverse the movements of Forms 35 and 36 by first stepping back on right leg and dropping right arm to waist height, palm up, and continuing movements on the left side (Fig. 48).

Then the left toes kick low to the left diagonal while the arms slide sideways, right hand at forehead height with palm out, and left forearm moving from elbow to the left (Fig. 49).

Seventh Series

38. TURN BODY AND KICK

Bringing left heel to upper inner right calf, move left arm across body to right, below waist with palm toward body; move the right

Fig. 48   Fig. 49

arm out and down in a low diagonal, and back slightly, body following (Fig. 50).

The right arm propels the body to the left and around in a sweeping half turn, pivoting on right heel.

Kick forward with left heel while right arm moves up to protect right temple and left arm strikes forward, palm open (Fig. 51).

39. BRUSH KNEE AND PUSH (left, then right)

Step forward and wide with left foot, heel first, toes forward. Simultaneously brush left hand across left knee and press forward with right fingers, as before.

Shift weight backward to right leg, brush right knee with right hand, turn left toes slightly outward, and shift weight to left foot. Step with right foot, heel first, toes forward, moving weight forward. With this step the left arm circles back and around and moves past left ear to press forward with fingertips, the right hand brushing across the right knee again (Fig. 52).

Fig. 50 Fig. 51

40. Step Forward and Punch to Opponent's Lower Abdomen

Weight shifts back to left leg, left arm lowers to side and right toes turn slightly outward. Step forward onto left leg, toes forward; brush left knee with left hand; punch forward with right fist to lower part of opponent's abdomen (Fig. 53).

After completing this form, repeat Forms 3, 4, 5, 6, and 7.

Eighth Series

41. Fair Lady Works at Shuttles *(left, right, left, and right)*

As the T'ai Chi player executes this form the hands move from left to right like the back-and-forth movement of a shuttle.

Fig. 52   Fig. 53

Shift weight to right leg and pivot on left heel as far right as possible while left arm moves across body at waist, palm up. Shift weight to left leg, continue movement to northeast corner by pivoting on right toes; the right arm moves slightly down toward left arm. Step with right foot (to northeast), then with left foot.

As weight shifts to left leg, left arm moves up to forehead, palm down, and fingertips of right hand press straight ahead to the left corner (Fig. 54).

Shift weight to right leg, pivot on left heel and turn right as far as possible while left arm moves slightly down to chin as before.

Shift weight to left foot, continuing movement to right by pivoting on right toes. Step with right foot to the right, making a three-quarter turn to the northwest corner. Lift right hand to forehead as before and press left fingertips forward while shifting weight onto right leg (Fig. 55).

Shift weight to left leg, step with right foot to southwest corner, right arm moving down toward waist.

Step in the same direction with left foot and press forward with right fingertips as left arm moves up to protect head, weight moving onto left foot. Right palm pushes through to the southwest corner (Fig. 56).

Shift weight to right leg, pivot on left heel to turn right, and slightly lower left arm. Shift weight to left leg and continue circling to right by pivoting on right toes.

Step right foot far around to complete three-quarter turn and face southeast corner, the right arm lifted to forehead and the left arm pressing forward, left toes turning inward (Fig. 57).

42. GRASP BIRD'S TAIL *(left)*

Repeat the movement described for Form 2; then repeat Forms 3, 4, 5, 6, and 7.

Ninth Series

43. SNAKE CREEPS DOWN

Repeat the movement described for Form 33.

Fig. 54

Fig. 55

Fig. 56

Fig. 57

44. STEP FORWARD, SEVEN STARS

In this form the hands are crossed at the wrists, resembling the seven-star constellation near the pole star.

As the body lifts, turn the right toes in and center the weight on left leg. Move the arms in front to upper chest height and form fists (with back of hands forward) that cross at the wrists, left wrist on inside of the right wrist. Simultaneously move the right foot on its toes in front of left heel (Fig. 58).

45. RIDE TIGER TO THE MOUNTAIN

As he executes this movement the player seems to be riding on a tiger.

Step back on right leg, move weight onto it, and drop left arm to left side. Circle the right hand out to side and up to forehead, palm a little down and forward. As arms move, bring left foot onto its toes in front of right heel (Fig. 59).

46. TURN BODY AND DO LOTUS KICK

A round flower with round leaves, the lotus seems to revolve when the wind blows. In this form the kick is delivered in a circular movement, reminding one of the revolving lotus leaves.

The left leg lifts off the ground slightly forward, and the body turns right to make a 360-degree turn on the ball of the right foot, the arms and legs giving the impetus to the movement (Fig. 60).

Drop right arm diagonally across body to left as far as it will naturally go, palm facing back. Simultaneously turn the left hand to face forward, moving the left arm forward slightly and circling out and back on the left diagonal.

Finish the turn with weight moved entirely onto left leg, knee bending deeply. Simultaneously move arms in front at chest height, palms down.

Lift right leg and touch toes to both palms, arms not moving (Fig. 61).

Fig. 58

Fig. 59

Fig. 60

Fig. 61

Tenth Series

47. Shoot Tiger

The two hands are held like a bow, the right hand above and the left below. The body and arms move from back to front, imitating the motion of an arrow.

Step forward on right leg and form fists with both hands, knuckles up, the left arm lowering slightly. Punch forward with both fists as the body moves forward (Fig. 62).

48. Circle Fist

Move weight back to left leg and drop arms to sides. Left arm stops at left side and right arm, making a fist, continues clockwise to hit the imagined opponent's head (Fig. 63).

Fig. 62

Fig. 63

Fig. 64

49. STEP FORWARD AND PUNCH

Put weight onto right leg, move left arm across body at chest level above the punching fist, and step forward with left foot. Then punch forward with right fist (Fig. 64).

50. CROSS HANDS—CONCLUSION OF T'AI CHI CH'UAN

Repeat the movement described for Form 17. Then, to conclude T'ai Chi Ch'uan, repeat Form 1.

IV. THE FORMS AND THE HEXAGRAMS

Beginning of the T'ai Chi Ch'uan

CHIN

The opening movement of T'ai Chi Ch'uan is derived from Hexagram 35, *Chin,* which represents Progress. This hexagram is composed of the upper trigram, *Li,* or sun, and the lower trigram, *K'un,* or earth: these elements together symbolize the sun rising above the earth. At the start of the day, the sun moves slowly higher and higher over the earth. This aspect of the sun's movement is captured in the first form.

The student stands erect as he begins the T'ai Chi Ch'uan. His legs are parallel to one another, the stance that is indicated by the lower nuclear trigram *Ken,* or legs (also, arms). His hands then rise slowly from his thighs in a parallel movement. This, too, is suggested by the trigram *Li,* with its two unbroken lines enclosing a broken line. The structure of this trigram calls to mind the epithet, "Strong outside, empty inside," a provocative description of the spiritually advanced man. The student's hands rise from his belly (the lower trigram, *K'un,* also means belly) to his shoulders and down again, slowly and gently.

In the Commentary on the Decision, a section of the *I Ching* in which the hexagrams are interpreted, the following comment is recorded: "Devoted, and clinging to this great clarity, the weak (or, gentle person) progresses and goes upward." This account of the *Chin* movement is further enhanced by the statement given as the Image of the hexagram:

> The sun rises over the earth:
> The image of Progress.
> Thus the superior man himself
> Brightens his bright virtue.

With this, the appropriateness of T'ai Chi Ch'uan is given yet another dimension: not only is it for health and self-defense, it is equally for the development of virtue.[1]

Grasp Bird's Tail and Push Up

CH'IEN

These forms originate with the first hexagram, *Ch'ien,* the Creative. The left palm is held at chin level as though grasping the head of the bird (or dragon). The right hand, placed to the side of the hip as though smoothing the bird's tail, then is raised to the bird's head. The *Book of Changes* says:

> Nine in the second place means:
> Dragon appearing in the field.

The number 9 indicates the unbroken line that is second from the bottom in the hexagram. The phrase "the second place" also refers to the abdomen. The line, "Dragon appearing in the field," is a concrete expression of the first statement, with the dragon represented by the hand and the field understood to be the abdomen.

As the hand, or dragon, flies upward to a place in front of the player's chin, the *Book of Changes* says:

> Nine in the fifth place means:
> Flying dragon in the heavens.

If the hand, however, rises too high and goes above the chin, we can speak of the hand as an arrogant dragon, and the movement becomes stiff and ungraceful.

Nine at the top means:
Arrogant dragon will have cause to repent.

Thus, Push Up reaches its end at the chin, or fifth place, and from there the new form begins.[2]

Pull Back

K'UN

The trigram *K'un,* the Receptive, characterizes Pull Back. The player's hands move downward from his upper right side toward his lower left. The opening words of the Great Commentary of the *I Ching* are appropriate: "Heaven is high, the earth is low."[3]

Press Forward

K'AN

This movement, related to the trigram *K'an,* finds the left hand placed on the right wrist, both hands positioned close to the chest. The hands then press forward, representing the new moon waxing to the full. But in the flow of nature, when the moon is full it begins to wane. The player then separates his hands and rests backward, indicating the waning moon.

Push Forward

LI

Based on the trigram *Li,* this form begins with the hands parallel to each other and in front of the body, a symbol of strength outside and emptiness within. The act of pushing forward recalls the arc of the sun as it goes forward across the heavens.

Push Up, Pull Back, Press Forward, and Push Forward also symbolize the four seasons. When these movements are completed, a new year begins with the transition to the Single Whip.

KO

Single Whip

The Single Whip comes from Hexagram 49, *Ko,* which means Revolution. According to the Commentary on the Decision, "Heaven and earth bring about revolution, and the four seasons complete themselves thereby." The nuclear trigrams *Ch'ien* (which means turning) and *Sun* (which means gentle and wind) suggest the essence of the movement: the body turning with hands still parallel almost 120 degrees from the termination of Push Forward, the previous movement. *Ch'ien* and *Sun* combined give the picture of the body rotating in a gentle flowing motion like a light wind.[4]

SUI

Play Guitar

Sui, Hexagram 17, which denotes Following, is related to Play Guitar *(right).* The upper trigram, *Tui,* may mean joyous or oval-shaped. The lower trigram, *Chen,* sometimes has the meanings of arousing or foot. The upper nuclear trigram, *Sun,* can denote wood or string. The lower nuclear trigram, *Ken,* signifies at times legs, arms, hands, or fingers.

By combining the various elements of the hexagram, we discover a picture of Play Guitar *(right). Tui* suggests a joyous activity, such as playing an instrument. The nuclear trigram *Sun* suggests the pi'pa, an ancient Chinese stringed instrument strummed like a guitar and constructed chiefly from wood. *Ken* indicates the fingers of the guitar-player.

Tui, insofar as it suggests the oval shape, signifies the hands of the combatant as he moves into a strong position, vigorously twisting the opponent's arm. The lower trigram, *Chen,* suggests a firm stance. The foot is aroused, lightly touching the floor and ready to kick.

The T'ai Chi player uses two hands to twist his opponent's arm, as the second line says:

> If one clings to the little boy,
> One loses the strong man.[5]

Step Forward and Strike with Shoulder

TA CHUANG

Step Forward and Strike with Shoulder is taken from Hexagram 34, *Ta Chuang,* which symbolizes the Power of the Great. The primary trigrams are *Chen,* which means arousing or thunder, and *Ch'ien,* which means strong, moving, or forward. The lower nuclear trigram is also *Ch'ien.* The upper is *Tui.* The four strong unbroken lines predominate within and at the lower part of the hexagram. The motion of Step Forward and Strike with Shoulder suggests a goat butting a fence or some like object. Thus the lines in the *I Ching* evoking the goat also evoke this form. In addition, *Tui,* the upper nuclear trigram, denotes goat as one of its multiple meanings. As the third line says:

> The inferior man works through power.
> The superior man does not act thus. . . .
> A goat butts against a hedge
> And gets its horns entangled.

To use Step Forward and Strike with Shoulder as a self-defense technique requires delicacy of aim. If the combatant's body is wrongly placed, the movement will be ineffective. As the Image states:

> Thus the superior man does not tread upon paths
> That do not accord with established order.[6]

White Crane Spreads Wings

PI

The T'ai Chi Ch'uan form White Crane Spreads Wings is based on Hexagram 22, *Pi*, which signifies Grace—beauty of form. The upper trigram, *Ken*, denotes hand or wing. The lower, *Li*, can mean bird or eye. In this form the hands become the crane's wings and one of them is placed above the eyes.

The upper nuclear trigram, *Chen*, suggests movement, feet or forest. When all of its lines are changed, *Chen* becomes *Sun*. Combining *Sun* with *Li*, we have the image of a white bird. The lower nuclear trigram, *K'an*, evokes the image of water. Thus, the hexagram gives the picture of a wild water bird on the outskirts of a forest, the white bird of this T'ai Chi movement.

The fourth line of Hexagram 22 mentions a white horse which comes as if on wings. But the hexagram itself suggests a flying bird, not a horse. The flying creature of the hexagram, with one wing *(Ken)* high and one low, resembles the actual posture of White Crane Spreads Wings.

Brush Knee and Push

KU

Ku, Hexagram 18, is related to Brush Knee and Push. The hexagram signifies Decay. More specifically *Ku* means to work on what has spoiled to remove the source of decay. *Ken*, the upper trigram, signifies hand, leg, or mountain. The lower trigram, *Sun*, means wind, gentle, or willow tree. The upper nuclear trigram is *Chen*, suggesting movement; the lower nuclear trigram is *Tui*. The combined images of the trigrams picture a man stepping forward and pushing. The Image which the *I Ching* gives for *Ku* states: ''The wind blows low on the mountain," another way of suggesting Brush Knee and Push.⁷ The mountain, of course, is derived from *Ken.* The lower trigram, *Sun,* governs the manner of the form: it is executed gently, like the wind blowing against a willow tree.

Brush Knee and Push is used in self-defense as a block against the kick or hand-blow of the opponent. As he blocks, the combatant points the fingers of his right hand at his opponent's throat.

Step Forward and Punch

YU

Step Forward and Punch comes from Hexagram 16, *Yu,* which denotes Enthusiasm. The upper trigram is *Chen,* meaning thunder, movement, and strength. The lower trigram, *K'un,* means earth or belly. The fourth line, the strong line, is like a fist placed at waist level. The upper nuclear trigram is *K'an,* meaning water or heart. It is appropriate to this movement in which the player punches out at the opponent's heart. The lower nuclear trigram, *Ken,* represents legs and arms, as well as mountain. The leg in Step Forward and Punch must stand firm like a mountain.

Chen often means foot. In relation to this T'ai Chi movement it signifies stepping forward, which is accomplished in a flowing motion, like running water. *K'an* means bow. The solid *yang* line is like an arrow, signifying the punch shot out like an arrow from a drawn bow.

In performing T'ai Chi Ch'uan this whole movement flows like *K'an,* water, and is soft like *K'un,* soil or earth. When Step Forward and Punch is used in an attack, however, it is quick like an arrow and powerful like thunder. Of course, an offensive movement such as this is used only when an attack was previously initiated by an opponent. Like all the techniques of T'ai Chi Ch'uan, this movement is not meant to be used aggressively but can be employed in self-defense.

MING I

Cross Hands

The Darkening of the Light, the theme of Hexagram 36, *Ming I,* is also the theme of Cross Hands. The upper trigram of the hexagram is *K'un,* the receptive, earth. The lower trigram, *Li,* means fire as well as light and signifies the sun sinking down beneath the earth. The upper nuclear trigram is *Chen,* which signifies movement or thunder. The three broken lines in the upper trigram mean that the two hands are separate as the movement begins. *Li,* with its broken line between the two unbroken ones, symbolizes the crossed hands, the position that is the goal of this movement. As the *Book of Changes* says:

> Six at the top means:
> Not light but darkness.
> First he climbed up to heaven,
> Then he plunged into the depths of the earth.

The hands rise and then come down to cross, at the end of the movement, before the chest.

The Beginning of the T'ai Chi Ch'uan is derived from the preceding hexagram, *Chin,* the sun rising from the earth. In contrast Cross Hands, which marks the end of the first section, is derived from *Ming I,* which signifies the sun sinking down over the earth.

As the Image puts it:

> Thus does the superior man live with the great mass:
> He veils his light, yet still shines.[8]

KEN

Bring Tiger to the Mountain

The *I Ching* Hexagram 52, *Ken,* which means Keeping Still, Mountain, is related to Bring Tiger to the Mountain. The upper and lower trigrams are both *Ken* and can signify arm or hand. The upper nuclear trigram, *Chen,* means embracing. The trigram *Ken* also sig- nifies tiger and mountain. Thus, the hexagram gives the image of a tiger embraced and related in some way to a mountain. The lower nuclear trigram is *K'an,* water. As he performs this movement, the T'ai Chi player seems to throw the tiger and then to let it go back to the mountain. Otherwise, he will be in danger. The Commentary on the Decision says:

> When it is time to stop, then stop.
> When it is time to advance, then advance.
> Thus movement and rest do not miss the right time.

Bring Tiger to the Mountain is the beginning of the second section of T'ai Chi Ch'uan. Sometimes the player stops before this form. When he feels ready to advance, he advances. The experienced student rests or continues at the right time.

> Mountains standing close together:
> The image of Keeping Still.
> Thus the superior man
> Does not permit his thoughts
> To go beyond his situation.[9]

Fist Under the Elbow

Fist Under the Elbow is derived from Hexagram 27, *I,* which denotes the Corners of the Mouth (Providing Nourishment). The hexagram is constructed from *Ken,* the upper trigram, which means hand or fingers and *Chen,* which indicates the feet, movement or arousing. Both nuclear trigrams are *K'un,* signifying belly, body, or hidden. In this form one foot is lightly placed with heel on the ground as suggested by the lower trigram, *Chen,* a foot ready for instanta- neous arousal, to kick whenever necessary.

In the Fourth Line we read: "Spying about with sharp eyes, like a tiger with insatiable craving."[10] These words suggest the spirit of the form which involves a scrupulous attention to the movements of the opponent as the combatant waits for an opening to strike a sudden blow with the fist or foot or open palm. These blows could be delivered simultaneously by a perfected T'ai Chi master.

Step Back and Repulse Monkey

TUN

Retreat, the essence of Hexagram 33, *Tun,* is also the essence of Step Back and Repulse Monkey. The upper trigram, *Ch'ien,* denotes movement. The lower trigram, *Ken,* means monkey, back, stop, and mountain. Combining the two trigrams, we find move or step back as one of the hexagram's possible meanings. Stop, or repulse, is also suggested by *Ken,* as well as monkey. This combination gives the whole form, Step Back and Repulse Monkey. The upper nuclear trigram, *Ch'ien,* means energy. The lower nuclear trigram, *Sun,* means gentle. Together they imply the gentle application of energy. As the Image says:

> Mountain under heaven: the image of Retreat . . .
> Not angrily but with reserve.

The Commentary on the Decision interprets further: " 'Retreat. Success': this means that success lies in retreating." The implications of this motif are drawn out in Book III of the *I Ching*.

The secret of the T'ai Chi Ch'uan lies in its refusal to use strength against strength. "Retreat and then wait for the right time to counterattack" is the essence of self-defense according to T'ai Chi.[11]

Slant Flying

HUAN

Huan, Hexagram 59, which means Dissolution, is related to Slant Flying. The upper trigram, *Sun,* connotes wind, penetration, or gentleness. The lower trigram, *K'an,* implies water, ear, or bow. The upper nuclear trigram is *Ken,* meaning leg, hand, or temple (of the head). The lower nuclear trigram is *Chen,* which means foot or movement. Taking the meanings movement (from *Chen*) and leg (from *Ken*), we have a forward step. The hand, as suggested by *Ken,* moves *(Chen)* to strike the opponent's ear *(K'an)* or temple *(Ken).*

Another interpretation is derived from an alternative meaning of the trigram *Sun:* chicken. Again, *K'an* denotes water or river. A chicken, flying slantingly to the sloping banks of a river, will fly low and must continue its trajectory until it finds flat ground or it will drown.

Needle at Sea Bottom

HSIAO KUO

Needle at Sea Bottom is taken from Hexagram 62, *Hsiao Kuo,* which means Preponderance of the Small. Taking the double broken and unbroken line couples as one unbroken line between two broken lines, we get *Big K'an,* which indicates a body of water. Waves piled up upon one another are signified by the double broken lines at the top of *Hsiao Kuo.* The broken lines below signify unfathomable depths. Together these elements give a picture of the sea.

The lower nuclear trigram, *Sun,* implies long, straight, or thread. The upper nuclear trigram, *Tui,* means metal and suggests a needle. Combining these two impressions, we have the form Needle at Sea Bottom.

The upper trigram of *Hsiao Kuo* is *Chen,* meaning movement, arousing, or foot. The lower, *Ken,* means leg or still. The nuclear hexagram is *Ta Kuo* (No. 28), meaning Preponderance of the Great. According to the Image of this hexagram, "The lake rises above the trees."[12] The water rises above the trees, long and straight *(Sun).* Water has risen above *Sun.* The needle has sunk to the bottom of the sea.

Play Arms Like a Fan

TA CH'U

Play Arms Like a Fan comes from Hexagram 26, *Ta Ch'u,* which means the Taming Power of the Great. The upper trigram is *Ken,* meaning small and hand, and the lower is *Ch'ien,* which means strong, firm, or great. A folding fan, for instance, can be both small and great. The upper nuclear trigram, *Chen,* meaning movement or bamboo, gives more substance to the image of the hands (from *Ken*) moving like a Chinese fan. The lower nuclear trigram, *Tui,* means hurt. One hand is utilized more than the other in the attack against the opponent.

The lower primary trigram, *Ch'ien,* means strong or firm, suggesting the posture of the T'ai Chi Ch'uan practitioner. His two hands rise like the upper nuclear trigram, *Chen. Ken,* the upper trigram, also means mountain. The Image, "Heaven within the mountain," gives the essence of the form.[13]

Turn Body and Strike Fist to Back

TA KUO

Hexagram 28, *Ta Kuo,* which means Preponderance of the Great, is related to Turn Body and Strike Fist to Back. The upper trigram, *Tui,* denotes lake or to smash. The lower trigram, *Sun,* means either gentle or wind. Both the upper and lower nuclear trigrams are *Ch'ien,* strong or turn. When the nuclear trigrams are changed to three unbroken lines, we have *K'un,* body. Taken together, the trigrams evoke the image of a body turning. The broken line at the top of *Tui* resembles a fist. According to the lines:

> Nine in the third place means:
> The ridgepole sags to the breaking point,

which implies that the fist is thrown back as the body turns.

When he uses this form for self-defense, as the opponent comes from behind, the T'ai Chi player turns around, throws his fist back and delivers a sharp blow to the opponent's head.

> Six at the top means:
> One must go through the water.
> It goes over one's head.

Tui implies water, as well as fist. The fist drops like rain on the opponent's head.

Ta Kuo, the hexagram of this form, is the nuclear hexagram of *Hsiao Kuo,* Hexagram 62, which is related to Needle at Sea Bottom. The lines of *Hsiao Kuo* state:

> Nine in the third place means:
> If one is not extremely careful,
> Somebody may come up from behind and strike him.[14]

Hit Tiger

Hit Tiger originates from Hexagram 42, *I,* which signifies Increase. The upper trigram, *Sun,* denotes gentleness or wind. The lower trigram, *Chen,* for purposes of this analysis signifies movement, foot, and arousing. The upper nuclear trigram is *Ken,* denoting arm, tiger, and temple. The lower nuclear triad is *K'un,* meaning ribs or quietness. Combining the trigrams for arm and movement, the signification is hitting. Adding to this picture the trigram for tiger, we have the T'ai Chi form Hit Tiger.

> Nine at the top means:
> . . . Indeed, someone even strikes him.[15]

The blow is delivered gently, as implied by *Sun* and *K'un.* As the one fist *(Ken)* strikes the temple (again, *Ken*), the other strikes the ribs *(K'un).*

Kick with Toes

This form and Hexagram 4, *Meng*, share the theme Youthful Folly. The upper trigram, *Ken*, means arm, leg, or mountain. The lower trigram, *K'an*, signifies danger or fetters. The upper nuclear trigram is *K'un*, meaning body or abdomen; the lower nuclear trigram is *Chen*, which means foot and arousing. *Chen* suggests one foot poised to kick. *Ken* suggests that the other foot, like a mountain, is placed solidly on the ground.

The kick is placed below the abdomen, in the genital region (suggested by *K'an*, water). The hands are raised in a block (suggested by the structure of *Ken*) as the kick is delivered. If the opponent catches the foot, the two fists are used to break his hold.

> Nine at the top means:
> In punishing folly
> It does not further one
> To commit transgressions.[16]

These lines, set down to elucidate the hexagram, are appropriate to Kick with Toes, which is used for defensive, not offensive, purposes.

Hit Opponent's Ears with Fists

Shih Ho, Hexagram 21, is the basis for this form. The meaning of the hexagram is Biting Through. The upper trigram is *Li*, signifying an arrow and suggesting, in its arrangement of lines, two parallel fists: "Strong outside, empty inside." The lower trigram is

Chen, meaning strength or movement. The upper nuclear trigram, *K'an,* signifies ear and danger. The lower nuclear trigram, *Ken,* meaning bow, arm, hand or forehead, combines with *K'an* to intensify the image of striking the ear or forehead.

> Nine at the top means:
> His neck is fastened in the wooden cangue,
> So that his ears disappear.
> Misfortune.[17]

The cangue, an ancient device for punishment, consists of two pieces of wood that grip the neck.

The upper primary trigram, *Li,* and the upper nuclear trigram, *K'an,* together form the image of the bow and arrow. The lower nuclear trigram, *Ken,* can mean legs and in this case indicates a step. The step results in one foot placed forward, bent like a bow, the other behind and straight like an arrow. Thus this form is the bow-and-arrow step of T'ai Chi.

Turn Body and Kick

WU WANG

The form Turn Body and Kick originates from Hexagram 25, *Wu Wang,* Innocence. The upper trigram, *Ch'ien,* means heaven, strength, energy, and to turn. The lower, *Chen,* means movement, foot, and to arouse. The upper nuclear trigram is *Sun,* meaning wind or gentleness. The lower nuclear trigram is *Ken,* which means firmness, leg or mountain.

The hexagram gives a picture of Turn Body and Kick. The player's body (*K'un,* derived by changing the lines of *Ch'ien*) turns (*Ch'ien*) and kicks (*Chen*) gently (*Sun*) like a light wind. *Ken* indicates one leg standing firmly like a mountain. According to the Image given for *Wu Wang,* "Under heaven thunder rolls."[18] When used for self-defense, the natural energy of this movement can be compared to the energy of thunder.

CHUN

Wave Hands Like a Cloud

This form is related to Hexagram 3, *Chun,* Difficulty at the Beginning. The upper trigram, *K'an,* means water, cloud, and wheel. The lower trigram, *Chen,* signifies thunder, wave, or horse. The upper nuclear trigram is *Ken,* meaning hands, arms, or legs. The lower nuclear trigram is *K'un,* indicating the belly or body.

Wave Hands Like a Cloud is built from the composite elements of the hexagram. Cloud comes from *K'an.* The hands *(Ken)* turn *(Chen)* like waves of water *(K'an)* or a wheel *(K'an).* The hands in motion pass across the belly *(K'un),* moving peacefully like clouds floating by in the sky.

> Clouds and thunder:
> The Image of Difficulty at the Beginning.
> Thus the superior man
> Brings order out of confusion.

The posture of the legs in this movement suggests a man mounted on a horse:

> Six in the second place means:
> Difficulties pile up.
> Horse and wagon part.[19]

SHIH

Snake Creeps Down

Hexagram 7, *Shih,* which means the Army, governs Snake Creeps Down. The upper trigram, *K'un,* signifies belly, body, or earth. The lower trigram, *K'an,* means water or snake. The upper nuclear trigram is also *K'un.* The lower nuclear trigram is *Chen,* which means movement and arousing.

The posture of the legs in this movement suggests a snake *(K'an)* creeping on the earth *(K'un).* The player's body is lowered so that the belly *(K'un)* is close to the knees.

The Image of *Shih* says,

> In the middle of the earth is water.

This form involves a kind of retreat from the hand- or foot- blows of the opponent. It is a subtle sinking backward like a strategic retreat by a cautious general.

> Six in the fourth place means:
> The army retreats. No blame.

According to the interpretation of this line: "In face of a superior enemy, with whom it would be hopeless to engage in battle, an orderly retreat is the only correct procedure, because it will save the army from defeat and disintegration. It is by no means a sign of courage or strength to insist upon engaging in a hopeless struggle regardless of circumstances."

The next movement, Golden Cock on One Leg, is more offensive. Thus the purpose of this retreat is to be able to advance later with more success.[20]

Golden Cock on One Leg

CHUNG FU

Golden Cock on One Leg is derived from Hexagram 61, *Chung Fu,* Inner Truth. The upper triad, *Sun,* means chicken or cock (as in the movement Slant Flying) as well as gentleness or wind. *Tui,* the lower trigram, signifies golden. The lower nuclear trigram is *Chen,* foot or arousing, whereas the upper is *Ken,* leg, hand, or mountain. The nuclear trigrams describe this movement: one leg is raised to strike with the knee *(Chen)* and the other is planted firmly on the ground like a mountain *(Ken).* The nuclear triads taken together also suggest that the hands are held above the leg.

High Pat on Horse

LU

This form comes from Hexagram 56, *Lu,* which means the wanderer. *Li,* the upper trigram, signifies "empty inside, strong outside" as well as horse and fire. *Ken,* the lower trigram, means keeping still, mountain, arm, or to pat. The upper nuclear trigram, *Tui,* means oval or to hurt. The lower nuclear trigram, *Sun,* means wind, gentleness, or high. Combining the trigrams we derive High *(Sun)* Pat *(Ken)* on Horse *(Li),* gently *(Sun).* As he works through this movement, the student places one hand slightly above the other so that a space remains between them. Thus the upper hand can suddenly strike the opponent's throat, reaching out in the arc suggested by *Tui,* hurting the opponent as indicated by the same trigram. Meanwhile, the lower hand grabs the combatant's hand *(Ken).*

Separate Feet and Kick

CHEN

The Arousing (Shock, Thunder) is the theme of this form and of Hexagram 51, *Chen.* Both the lower and upper trigrams are *Chen,* meaning to arouse, movement, and foot. The upper nuclear trigram, *K'an,* means water flowing or danger.

The primary trigrams *(Chen)* and the lower nuclear trigram *(Ken)* suggest the hand and leg movements of this form. One foot is poised for kicking *(Chen),* the other is solidly placed *(Ken).* The kick is delivered in a flowing manner, like water *(K'an).*

The Image of this hexagram states:

Thunder repeated: the image of Shock.[21]

Separate Feet and Kick when performed in practice is like flowing water *(K'an).* But in self-defense the movement becomes thunder

(Chen) from the hands and feet. The kick, delivered to the opponent's shin, shocks him like a clap of thunder.

CH'IEN

Step Forward and Punch to Opponent's Lower Abdomen

Step Forward and Punch finds its base in Hexagram 15, *Ch'ien,* which means Modesty. The upper trigram, *K'un,* denotes earth, belly, or abdomen. The lower trigram, *Ken,* means mountain, leg, or arm. The upper nuclear trigram is *Chen* and signifies movement or strength. The lower nuclear trigram is *K'an,* water or danger.

The third line from the bottom of the hexagram, the highest line in *Ken,* signifies a fist. The only strong line in the hexagram, it is placed below the abdomen *(K'un).* The lower nuclear trigram, *K'an,* signifies the genital area, a place of danger if one is attacked.

Taken together the trigrams mean stepping forward to punch below the abdomen.

Modesty is the character of this hexagram. It indicates the gentle, nonaggressive stance of T'ai Chi Ch'uan. This does not mean, of course, that the T'ai Chi practitioner will shy away from force when force is called for.

> Six in the fifth place means:
> . . . It is favorable to attack with force.

Force is used, according to the *I Ching,* "in order to chastise the disobedient."[22]

CHIEH

Fair Lady Works at Shuttles

Hexagram 60, *Chieh,* is related to this form. *Chieh* signifies Limitation. The upper trigram, *K'an,* means water, turn, or wheel. The lower trigram, *Tui,* denotes a fair lady. The upper nuclear trigram is *Ken,* which means mountain, arm, leg, or hand. The lower nuclear trigram is *Chen,* meaning movement, strength, or wood, and suggesting the moving wood of a shuttle. *Chen* also means to cut and left. Combined with *Tui,* which also means right and oval-shaped, these trigrams set the image of a shuttle moving from left to right.

In executing this form, the player's body turns around again and again like a water wheel (suggested by *K'an*). The body turns a total of four times, the number of seasons in the year. The Commentary on *Chieh* includes these appropriate words: "Heaven and earth have their limitations, and the four seasons of the year arise."[23]

The turns in this form must be accomplished smoothly, like flowing water *(K'an).* When used for defense purposes, one hand blocks and the other pushes forward offensively.

Step Forward, Seven Stars

FENG

Step Forward, Seven Stars originates from Hexagram 55, *Feng,* Abundance. The upper trigram, *Chen,* means foot or arousing. The lower trigram, *Li,* signifies fire, sun, or eye. The upper nuclear trigram is *Tui,* which means to hurt. The lower nuclear trigram is *Sun,* gentleness or strength.

One foot, in accordance with *Chen,* is aroused and ready to kick. The one broken line of *Tui* symbolizes the two fists before the chest. *Sun* means that the motions in this movement are executed gently. *Li* signifies the sun, the star of our solar system. When the Judgment reads, "Be like the sun at midday," it refers to the two fists in the middle of the chest.

> Six in the second place means:
> . . . That the polestars can be seen at noon.

The polestars are a cluster of seven stars, and their mention in this statement relates the hexagram to the movement, Step Forward, Seven Stars.

The lower nuclear trigram, *Sun,* can also mean forward and backward. "It is advance and retreat." The Commentary on the hexagram points out the waxing and waning flow of events in nature: "When the sun stands at midday, it begins to set." This leads to Ride Tiger to the Mountain, a form of retreat.[24]

Ride Tiger to the Mountain

Chien, Hexagram 53, is the basis in the *I Ching* for Ride Tiger to the Mountain. The hexagram means Development. The upper trigram, *Sun,* signifies gentleness and wind. The lower trigram, *Ken,* means mountain, arm, leg, and tiger. The upper nuclear trigram is *Li,* meaning arrow, and the lower nuclear trigram is *K'an,* meaning bow. The broken line of *Sun* symbolizes the student's two legs. With the meanings mountain and tiger from *Ken,* the two trigrams together yield this T'ai Chi form.

Turn Body and Do Lotus Kick

WEI CHI

This movement is taken from Hexagram 64, *Wei Chi,* Before Completion. The upper trigram, *Li,* means sun, fire, and eyes. The lower trigram, *K'an,* signifies water, wheel, turn, and devil. The upper nuclear trigram is also *K'an* and the lower is, again, *Li.* Turn *(K'an)* the whole body like a wheel *(K'an).*

> Nine in the fourth place means:
> Perseverance brings good fortune.
> Remorse disappears.
> Shock, thus to discipline the Devil's Country.[25]

The shock refers to the kick, delivered to the middle section of the opponent's body. *K'an* also means kidney, which is known in this Taoist system as "the Devil's Country."

Shoot Tiger

HSIEH

Deliverance, the meaning of Hexagram 40, *Hsieh*, is the rationale for Shoot Tiger. The upper trigram, *Chen*, signifies movement, strength, thunder, and foot. The lower trigram, *K'an*, means water, wheel, bow, rain, and danger. The lower nuclear trigram is *Li*, meaning arrow.

We have, by combining *Li* and *K'an*, the image of the bow and arrow. *Chen*, when inverted, becomes *Ken*, which has the meanings of tiger and arm. And these trigrams give the image of shooting the tiger. Two fists are pressed forward (from *Chen*, movement). *Li* signifies that the arrows are aimed at the opponent's temple and ribs. According to the Commentary on the Decision of *Hsieh:* "Danger (from *K'an*) produces movement *(Chen)*. Through movement one escapes danger: this is deliverence."[26]

Circle Fist

TING

Circle Fist is taken from Hexagram 50, Ting, the Caldron. The upper trigram, *Li*, means weapon, eyes, and suggests the aphorism, "Strong outside, empty inside." The lower trigram, *Sun*, signifies wood, gentleness, and strength. The upper nuclear trigram is *Tui*, which means smash, hurt, or right. The lower nuclear trigram is *Ch'ien*.

The fists of this form are suggested by the top line of *Tui*. The lower trigram, *Sun*, denotes the two feet standing firmly. The player circles his fist to smash *(Tui)* the opponent's head *(Ch'ien)*.

At the end of the second section, the form Cross Hands, based on Hexagram 36, *Ming I*, is repeated. The return to *Ming I*, Darkening of the Light, means that this section of movements can be compared to the cycle of the sun as it moves from one horizon to the next. To conclude the section Form 1, the Beginning of the T'ai Chi Ch'uan, derived from *Chin* (the sun rising), is repeated. The whole cycle of movements can then be repeated from the beginning, as the sun rising and setting once more.

CHIN

MING I

V. THE TAO OF SELF-DEFENSE

This subject is different from the martial arts, for a number of reasons. First, T'ai Chi is the Tao. In the Great Treatise Ta Ch'uan of the *I Ching* it says: "That which lets now the dark, now the light appear, is tao." Second, T'ai Chi Ch'uan is the movement of the Tao. Lao-tzu says, "The motion of the Tao is cyclical. The way of the Tao is pliant." Third, the principles of the T'ai Chi Ch'uan emanate from Taoist philosophy.

T'ai Chi Ch'uan is derived from the Taoist system of self-defense in that it does not emphasize specific techniques. Other disciplines are learned through the mastery of various techniques—such as kicks, blocks, and punches. Specific attacks are met with specific answers. This is not the case with T'ai Chi Ch'uan. Although T'ai Chi Ch'uan seeks to train the body, it does so in order to cultivate an attitude, a state of mind, an understanding. It is this attitude that is most important in defeating an opponent, not merely the techniques employed. To understand this attitude, it is necessary for us to go to its source, and that source is the *Tao Teh Ching:*

> The best warrior is not warlike.
> The best fighter is not angry.
> The best winner does not compete.

This is central to the practice of T'ai Chi Ch'uan. Just as the forms are performed in an easy and calm manner, so must one meet an opponent gently and humbly, always with peaceful intent. Even in extreme danger the situation must be met with neither rage nor fear. The best T'ai Chi masters always possess this gentle manner and evenness of mind. This is quite different from those who practice other disciplines that are strenuously violent, and who imitate the arrogant gestures of wild animals to lead other people to believe what fierce, strong, and brave men they are. Lao-tzu says:

It has been said that he who knows how to preserve life avoids the rhinoceros and tiger when travelling by land; dodges arms and weapons when engaged in battle with a hostile army. He sees to it that the rhinoceri have no opportunity to use their horns; that tigers have no opportunity to use their claws; that enemies have no opportunity to use their weapons. Why is this so? Because man avoids the risks of death.

Tao Teh Ching

For all their strength and ferocity the tiger and rhinoceros cannot hurt a fly, because a fly cannot be torn by the tiger's claws or impaled on the horn of the rhinoceros. Similarly, a very sharp weapon cannot cut a feather in the air. The practitioner of T'ai Chi seeks to be like the fly and the feather. The body of a T'ai Chi master is always perfectly relaxed and calm, capable of responding to the slightest stimulus. One T'ai Chi master, Yang Lu Chan, could put a bird in the palm of his hand, and when the bird tried to fly, would relax his palm; the bird, lacking support, would not be able to fly.

The way of the Tao, then, is a gentle way, a way of humbleness and inaction. T'ai Chi Ch'uan follows these same precepts. It is a system geared specifically for defense. Lao-tzu writes:

> In strategy: defend rather than attack
> Retreating a foot is better than advancing an inch.
> This is action without acting
> Rolling up the sleeves without showing the arms.

The strength of the T'ai Chi Ch'uan is its ability to yield, and not in its ability to attack. When facing an opponent, it is his moves that guide our own. The hands and the forearms are used, gently, rather than the biceps and shoulders. In the classic treatise on T'ai Chi Ch'uan by Wang Chung-yueh, he describes this principle: "When the opponent employs a hard force, and I, a soft one, such a move is termed 'moving away' (Tsou)." Force is never answered by force.

It is obvious, however, that any system of self-defense must incorporate offensive techniques in order to overcome an opponent.

Thus, when the opponent has expended his force, the practitioner of T'ai Chi Ch'uan must be prepared to take advantage and strike quickly:

When one wishes to expand one must first contract. When one wishes to be strong, one must first be weak. When one wishes to rise, one must first fall. When one wishes to take, one must first give. This is called mere truism. Meekness can overcome strength.

Tao Teh Ching, Cheng Lin translation

Especially essential are the writings of Chuang-tzu (*Texts of Taoism,* part 1, pp. 198–200). Here Chuang-tzu tells the story of Wanhui's cook, who butchered oxen for his master.

Whenever he applied his hand, leaned forward with his shoulder, planted his foot, and employed the pressure of his knee, in the audible ripping off of the skin, and slicing operation of the knife, the sounds were all in regular cadence. Movements and sounds proceeded as in the dance of "the Mulberry Forest."

The above passage corresponds to several movements of T'ai Chi Ch'uan. "Applied his hand" refers to forms such as Pull, Push, and Press. "Leaned forward with his shoulder" is Strike with Shoulder and "pressure on his knees" corresponds to Golden Cock Stands on One Leg. The reference to musical dance describes the smoothness, gracefulness, balance, and harmony of the T'ai Chi movements.

Later, when the cook finished, the ruler said:

"That your art should have become so perfect!" [Having finished his operation], the cook laid down his knife, and replied to the remark, "What your servant loves is the method of the Tao, something in advance of any art."

The ruler observed that his strokes were so beautiful and gentle that he had reached the pinnacle of his art, but the cook was not satisfied with this praise and replied that his method was the Tao, beyond any of the arts. Here is the principle of the Tao of self-defense, which is quite different from any of the martial arts. The cook continued:

After three years I ceased to see it as a whole. Now I deal with it in a spirit-like manner, and do not look at it with my eyes. The use of my senses is discarded, and my spirit acts as it wills.

When the T'ai Chi player reaches a certain point, he should focus his mind like an archer or marksman, using his eyes, ears, and mind to observe the intention of his opponent. Later in the second stage the player should use his spirit and diminish the use of his senses. Finally he will be able to apply his spirit entirely as he wishes.

Then the cook explains how to use this technique:

Observing the natural lines, [my knife] slips through the great crevices and slides through the great cavities, taking advantage of the facilities thus presented. My art avoids the membranous ligatures, and much more the great bones.

T'ai Chi is comparable to the flow of water. When meeting an obstacle in a stream, it withdraws and eddies and swirls away finally again to seep and flow past at a different angle or to come back as waves, so finally overcoming the obstacle to its progress. In T'ai Chi Ch'uan this ebb and flow is neutralization and counterattack.

The cook further remarks:

A good cook changes his knife every year;—[it may have been] injured in cutting; an ordinary cook changes his every month;—[it may have been] broken. Now my knife has been in use for nineteen years; it has cut up several thousand oxen, and yet its edge is as sharp as if it has newly come from the whetstone.

This passage is a metaphor for a master who fought for nineteen years but was never injured by his opponents. The ancient Taoist said:

If you want to be immortal, first comes longevity, if you want longevity, then there must be no weakness or sickness, and finally to avoid sickness, avoid injury.

Chuang-tzu in another chapter said:

You must be still; you must be pure; not subjecting your body to toil, not agitating your vital force;—then you may live for long.
[Part II, Section IV, p. 298.]

Finally the cook reveals the method of the attack when meeting the difficult opponent. He says:

Nevertheless, whenever I come to a complicated joint, and see that there will be some difficulty, I proceed anxiously and with caution, not allowing my eyes to wander from the place, and moving my hand slowly. Then by a very slight movement of the knife, the part is quickly separated, and drops like [a clod of] earth to the ground.

This passage teaches the player to concentrate his mind and with a slow, precise movement defeat his opponent without the opponent realizing how he was defeated.

Finally the ruler exclaims:

The ruler Wan-hui said, "Excellent! I have heard the words of my cook, and learned from them the nourishment of [our] life."

The above passage from Chuang-tzu's writing emphasizes the same idea for good health that Master Chang San-feng emphasizes in the *T'ai Chi Ch'uan Lun*. Defense is secondary to the main purposes of prolonging life and youth.

In the first edition of this book, only six pages, entitled "T'ai Chi Ch'uan Used for Self-defense," referred to self-defense. Many readers thought it was not detailed enough. In this edition I introduce the philosophy of Lao-tzu and Chuang-tzu for the principle of self-defense. If we follow the principle and practice correctly the forms that make the body and mind relax—for instance, by practicing Push Hand carefully—one can understand the opponent's motive, neutralize his force, and counterattack. Furthermore, the student should understand the idea of the *T'ai Chi Ch'uan Classics* and remember all the principles. When one either practices forms or Push Hands and applies the purpose skillfully, one can defeat rivals under any conditions.

T'ai Chi Ch'uan Used for Self-Defense

I have discovered that there are many misconceptions about the use of T'ai Chi Ch'uan for self-defense. Westerners usually regard T'ai Chi as only a health exercise, or else they assume that it is simply a variation of Karate or Judo. The T'ai Chi Ch'uan system does contain self-defense forms which originated in the Taoist competition with the

Buddhist form of Shiao-lin boxing. This competition is spoken of in many of the older legends and stories from Chinese history.

Self-defense naturally involves rapid hand and leg movements that are quite a bit faster than the movements used when T'ai Chi is practiced alone. Although this is true, the spirit of self-defense in T'ai Chi is identical to the spirit used in executing the forms. It is relaxed and smooth, without anxiety or pride. Its particular flavor is best exemplified by the *I Ching* aphorism, "Only through the divine can one hurry without haste and reach the goal without walking."[1] Even in self-defense one must learn to abide in the Tao.

After becoming skilled in the practice of the forms, the next step is to learn to push hands. This involves the four fundamental forms: Push Up, Pull Back, Press Forward, and Push Forward. Pushing hands reinforces or corrects the student's execution of the forms, at the same time that it is the first step in the practice of self-defense. It makes the player more balanced and pliable. One learns the opponent's intentions from actual contact with him.

SINGLE PUSH HAND

Two opponents stand face to face, two steps apart. Each steps forward on his right foot and raises his right arm so that the opponents' wrists touch with palms turned inward to the chest. Then a circular movement is transacted by the arms as they move forward and backward with the wrists still touching. The left feet are then brought forward and the left hands perform a similar movement.

DOUBLE PUSH HANDS

When the second opponent *(B)* raises his right arm to resist the first opponent *(A)*, *A* places his palms on *B*'s right arm and pushes forward against *B*'s chest (Fig. 65). *B* raises his arms with *A*'s palms still adhering to his right arm. *B* is now ready to counterattack.

A pushes forward and shifts his weight to the right foot and puts his left hand on his own right wrist, pressing forward against *B* (Fig. 66). *B* turns his body, shifts to left foot, raises his right arm, elbow touching *A*'s arm, and then pulls to the left side. The left hand pushes

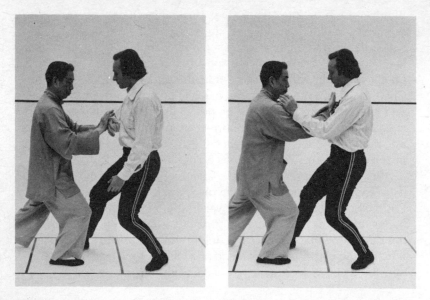

Fig. 65   **Fig. 66**

A's elbow and the right hand pushes his wrist, continuing to push up and press forward.

When A is pressed by B's movements forward, he shifts his weight to the left leg, raising his right arm, with his elbow touching B's arm (Fig. 67). At the same time he sinks back slightly with his elbow turned to the left rear to neutralize B's force. Then A's right hand moves down and around B's right hand and leads it to the side. A's right hand crosses and pushes against the wrist while the left hand pushes the elbow or forearm (Fig. 68).

Then push forward as in Fig. 65 and press forward as in Fig. 66.

MOVING DOUBLE PUSH HANDS

In the previous Push Hand forms, the lower body remains fixed, while the upper body moves back and forth. In Moving Push Hands, the hand movements continue while the legs move backward and forward in coordination with the hand movements.

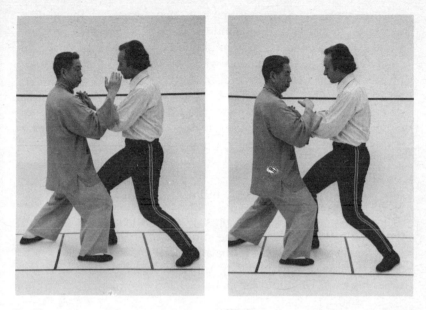

Fig. 67   **Fig. 68**

A and *B* push hands as described in Double Push Hands. Continuing these movements, *A* takes one step forward, and at the same time *B* takes one step backward (*A* advances toward *B* while *B* retreats). This is repeated, each time adding an additional step. Three steps are sufficient.

TA LU

The next practice step is called *Ta Lu*. At the same time that *A* makes one step forward and another sideward, *B* steps backward and retreats one step to the side. Thus, all four corners of an imaginary square in which the opponents practice are covered by their steps. Besides the hand movements Push Up, Pull Back, and Press Forward, *Ta Lu* also includes other movements. All together *Ta Lu* consists of eight moves which correspond to the eight trigrams of the *I Ching*.

When these self-defense forms have been mastered, the student can begin to learn Hand-to-Hand Combat, also known as Separate Hand. This is a complete system of hand combat which consists of eighty-eight distinct movements with variations, utilizing each form of the T'ai Chi Ch'uan. Several of these movements are demonstrated in Figs. 69–74. The step-by-step mastery of T'ai Chi for self-defense is comparable to learning the *I Ching,* which precedes from understanding the eight trigrams to mastery of the sixty-four hexagrams with their 384 lines.

NEEDLE AT SEA BOTTOM (FIG. 69)

If the opponent strikes with his fist or holds your wrist, grasp his wrist and pull it down, using the intrinsic force and weight of your trunk and legs. He will lose his balance and fall forward. If he resists or lifts his arms upward, use Play Arms Like a Fan to lift his arms and strike his waist with your left palm.

SNAKE CREEPS DOWN (FIG. 70)

If the opponent strikes with his fist high, Snake Creeps Down can be used to escape the blow.

Fig. 69

Fig. 70

Fig. 71

Fig. 72

Fig. 73

Fig. 74

GOLDEN COCK ON ONE LEG (FIGS. 71, 72, 73)

After retreating from the opponent with the form Snake Creeps Down, one of these variations of Golden Cock on One Leg can be used to counterattack. In Fig. 71 the left arm lifts the opponent's elbow while the right knee strikes his lower abdomen. In Figs. 72 and 73 the right arm grasps the opponent's arm to hold him in range while the left hand thrusts at his throat. Simultaneously, in Fig. 72 the right foot kicks the opponent's leg, while in Fig. 73 the right knee is used against his lower abdomen.

STEP FORWARD AND PUNCH (FIG. 74)

This form can also be adapted to avoid the opponent's high punch. The left arm raises the opponent's arm at the elbow while the right fist punches his abdomen. At the same time as the punch is executed, the step is taken to increase the punching arm's forward thrust.

VI. TAOIST MEDITATION AND T'AI CHI CH'UAN

The highest goal in Taoism is to reach a state of consciousness which transcends the bonds of mortality that cramp ordinary existence. This state is the Tao. The achievement of the Tao can be realized only after a long process of insight and concentration. The subtle process of Taoist meditation is exceedingly complex and varies from one master to another. Accuracy and resultant progress depend on the degree of enlightenment of the master who supervises the process.

Taoist meditation can be thought of as an alchemical procedure. It involves the refinement of one psychic substance into another. The process begins with *ching,* or sexual energy. *Ching* is converted into another substance, *chi,* when it is combined with the breath in a certain way. The purification of *chi* results in its transformation to *shen,* or spirit. In the last stage *shen* is converted to *shu,* or emptiness. T'ai Chi Ch'uan gives an outer image of the inner transformations of Taoist meditation. The T'ai Chi movements are paradigms of the inner processes that take place in Taoist alchemy.

When a metal is to be transformed by alchemy, it is usually heated for a period of time in a special flask. The heating process is repeated several times. Then the purified substance is passed to another flask where it is transformed in a new way. A bellows is used frequently by the alchemist to regulate the temperature and intensity of the fire.

The body of the student of Taoist meditation can be compared to the alchemist's laboratory. The psychic centers, or spiritual organs, of the body have the function of the flasks in alchemical distillation. The breath of the meditator can be compared to the bellows and the psychic fluid to the elixir which is passed from one flask to another in the laboratory.

In our bodily laboratory, then, we have twelve flasks, or psychic centers. In Taoist symbolism these centers are referred to as months of the year or constellations of the zodiac. Each one of these points can be represented by a hexagram of the *I Ching*. For instance, the point at the base of the spine, known as *wei lu* or the Gate of the Tail, corresponds to the hexagram *Fu;* the psychic center located in the brain and known as *ni wan* corresponds to the hexagram *Ko.*

As meditation begins the *ching,* or sexual energy, is moved upward to a point about an inch and a half below the navel. This may be compared to the process of heating a caldron on a stove. The point is known as the *tan tien.* At the *tan tien* the first purification cycle begins. This cycle is known as the Lesser Heavenly Circulation and is elegantly described by the first T'ai Chi Ch'uan movement.

From an erect position, with knees slightly bent, arms at sides with palms facing backward, both hands are slowly raised to the level of the shoulders and then slowly pressed down to the original position, as though an invisible force were pulling them up and down. As the hands are raised, the breath is drawn in and as they are lowered, it is exhaled. In this movement the *chi* is experienced as rising from the *tan tien* and then descending back to it as the arms are raised and lowered. When breathing in, the *chi* moves up in the front of the body; when breathing out, it moves down. This up-and-down movement is sometimes poetically referred to as the union of *Li* and *K'an,* fire and water. *K'an,* which means water, refers to the region of the lower abdomen, which is known as the Seat of Water. It also refers to the psychic center of this region. *Li,* on the other hand, which means fire, refers to the region of the heart and its corresponding spiritual center. Passion, which springs from the heart region, can appropriately be compared to fire and this region is often known as the Seat of Fire. Thus, the first T'ai Chi movement describes a process of ascent and descent between these two regions until the elixir slips back into the *tan tien.* The subtle substance is now ready for its next step of purification, known as the Greater Heavenly Circulation.

The Greater Heavenly Circulation is a purification cycle that passes the *chi* through all the psychic centers. *Ching* has already been transformed to *chi* by its admixture with breath during the Lesser Heavenly Current. The *chi* must now pass through the two main channels: one in front of the body, known as *Jen Mu* or the "involuntary course," and one in the back called *Tu Mu* or the "controlled course." *Tu Mu* is comprised of the psychic centers known respectively as *wei lu* (at the tip of the spine), *shun fu* (slightly below the middle of the spine), *hsuan shu* (in the middle of the spine), *chai chi* (slightly above the middle of the spine), *t'ao tao* (below the neck), *yu chen* (in the back of the head), *ni wan* (crown of the head), and *ming t'ung* (between the eyebrows). *Tu Mu* ends at the upper lip. *Jen Mu* begins in the lower lip and passes through *t'an chung* (in the chest), *chung huan* (above the navel), *shen chueh* (in the navel), and *ch'i hai* (about three inches below the navel).

The Greater Heavenly Circulation is captured in the Tai Chi Ch'uan form Step Back and Repulse Monkey. In this form the movement of the *chi* is described by the movement of the player's hands. The right hand drops to the region of the thigh, moves back and rises to the top of the head, and then is pushed forward and down, returning to the starting point. The left hand describes the same movements. However, when the right hand is at the top of the head, the left hand is in the thigh region. The relation of the two hands can be thought of as two diametrically opposed spokes of a wheel, while the movement of the wheel itself signifies the orbiting of the *chi* through the Greater Heavenly Circulation.

These are not the only orbits used in meditation for purposes of purification of the elixir. T'ai Chi Ch'uan describes several other orbits. For instance, a series of forms beginning with White Crane Spreads Wings illustrates a related but more extensive movement than the Lesser Heavenly Current. As the student executes the White Crane movement, the right hand guides the *chi* from the *tan tien* in the abdomen to the *ming t'ung,* the center between the eyes. Then the right hand brings the *chi* down again to the abdomen. The circulation of *chi* is continued in the next form, Brush Knee and Push, where the *chi* is brought down below the abdomen to the genital region and then up again until it reaches the throat center. The *chi* is brought down again, in the form Needle at Sea Bottom, to the genital region. The *chi* is then raised as the hands move apart in Play Arms Like a Fan. In this form *chi* is brought back through the *ming t'ung,* through the *ni wan* to the top of the head and then down again.

Another orbit of the *chi* is demonstrated by the movement Wave

Hands Like a Cloud. In meditation this orbit is conceived within a plane inside the belly. In the T'ai Chi form the left hand guides the *chi* from the upper left down to the right side of the body. Then the right hand starts from the lower left and moves in a graceful circle to the upper right, then down again to the right.

Whereas Wave Hands Like a Cloud describes an unusual orbit of the *chi* in the front of the belly, the form Fair Lady Works at Shuttles describes a similarly unusual orbit which circulates from the front of the belly to the back. Then the orbit itself pivots on its axis and the *chi* takes a similar but opposite course throughout the body. In the form itself there are two pivots to the right and two to the left. The orbit of the *chi* is elliptical and turns on an axis which is tilted in a northeasterly angle to the vertical.

From the upper left, the left hand sweeps downward to the right, describing the *chi* moving downward in the arc in the front of the belly. The body then pivots to the left, indicating an epicycle formed after the *chi* passes into the base of the dorsal region. The left hand, now at the right bottom, then sweeps upward and to the left, retracing the original arc of the *chi* back through the familiar orbit. The right hand is then pushed forward, bringing the *chi* down to the right as the body then pivots to the left and the right hand then channels the *chi* upward to the left. In the next two parts of the form, the body pivots to the right and the *chi,* in general, passes up through the top of the head, makes its little epicycle and passes down again. This passage is signified by the hands moving up, the body pivoting, and the hands moving down again.

Besides demonstrating the circulation of *chi,* T'ai Chi Ch'uan is related to classic Chinese sitting meditation in a number of ways. Both require keeping the torso erect but relaxed, the head erect, the neck straight, the arms and legs curved, and the shoulders down with the arms relaxed. The mind, in both cases, must be clear and still. Both require "right effort," a kind of effortless concentration free of goals or pride. In T'ai Chi the body moves outside and is still inside; in sitting meditation there must be stillness within and without. Breathing is an essential part of T'ai Chi and meditation; but in T'ai Chi breathing is assisted by the body's movement, whereas in meditation the breath is controlled solely by the mind.

T'ai Chi Ch'uan can be considered a kind of preparatory exercise for meditation, although, of course, it can be studied for a variety of other reasons. It disciplines the body, teaches relaxation and clear-headedness, accustoms the student to regulated breathing, and demonstrates the circulation of *chi* by a method far more close to the real event of meditation than looking at diagrams or hearing oral descriptions. More than that, T'ai Chi Ch'uan gives something of the spirit of meditation, a spirit which, in our overactive, anxiety-ridden lives, we seldom taste in day-to-day living—a spirit which promises a glimpse of peace beyond the scope of our present imagination or our ordinary understanding of the world.

VII. THE T'AI CHI CH'UAN CLASSICS

The T'ai Chi Ch'uan Classics are important texts for the practitioner where the principles and key instructions are provided. They state the basic rules of T'ai Chi Ch'uan. Some T'ai Chi Ch'uan schools that have been formed recently contradict one another because they do not follow this treatise.

My translation of the *Classics* is included in this expanded edition of *T'ai Chi Ch'uan and I Ching* as an aid to understanding the ideas and principles discussed in this work. When the practices of a T'ai Chi Ch'uan practitioner differ from these *Classics,* their forms will be incorrect.

Among the many texts, three classics stand out in importance. The first work is *T'ai Chi Ch'uan Lun,* or *Analects of T'ai Chi Ch'uan,* which is credited to Chang San-feng, the founder of T'ai Chi Ch'uan. The second work is *T'ai Chi Ch'uan Ching,* or *Treatise of T'ai Chi Ch'uan,* which is credited to Wang Chung-yueh, an enlightened master of the Ming Dynasty. The third text is called *Elucidation of the Thirteen Postures,* the authorship of which is disputed. Some credit it to Wang Chung-yueh; others to Wu Yu-hsiang, a scholarly T'ai Chi master of the Ch'ing Dynasty. In any case, this work is a classic to be used by the practitioner. The last text is *The Song of the Thirteen Postures,* which summarizes the meaning of the Thirteen Postures in song form, making it easier to memorize. Each treatise discusses form, *chi,* health, and self-defense. The first treatise concentrates mostly on a description of the form, the fundamental elements of the forms, and health; the second treatise emphasizes philosophy and defense. In the third treatise, there is more emphasis on *chi.*

The *T'ai Chi Ch'uan Lun,* by Chang San-feng

Each movement, in every part of the body should be light and agile. More important, each part must be articulated [linked] like a string of pearls.

In T'ai Chi Ch'uan, the body, the movements, and the *chi* must be coordinated like the T'ai Chi symbol, the T'ai Chi Tu. This principle has a scientific basis. The body can be compared with a machine. Each part must move smoothly and effortlessly, producing effective and economic results. For example, a car or plane operates in a light and effortless manner. They can both carry heavy weights and travel vast distances. Just as it is important that no part of a machine be loose or defective, it is equally important that the T'ai Chi Ch'uan movements be continuous and relaxed. If applied as a method of self-defense, T'ai Chi Ch'uan has no match.

The *chi* [breath] must be still inside; it must penetrate all the body. The spirit [energy] should be concentrated and hidden within.

In T'ai Chi Ch'uan, the *chi* (breath) should be stimulated. The *shen* (spirit/vitality) should be concentrated inward. There are two kinds of *chi;* one is outside (air/breathing); the other is inside (oxygen/blood circulation). The Chinese word *ku* means "act" or "stimulate"; the word *tuang* means "react." In the beginning "breathe in" is *ku,* "act," and "breathe out" is *tuang,* "react." In the second step, the *chi* can reach below the navel to the *tan tien.* This is described in the t'ai chi symbol (see Fig. 75) as follows:

The white circle in the middle represents the *tan tien.* The trigram K'an at the bottom of the circle represents the abdomen. The middle line of K'an is *yang* and represents the pre-natal breath, which rises from the abdomen along the *yang* (white) line to the navel. The trigram Li at the top of the circle represents the heart. The middle line of Li is *yin* and represents the post-natal breath, which descends from the heart along the *yin* (black) line to the *tan tien.*

When the practitioner breathes in, the air goes down to the *tan tien.* At the same time the pre-natal breathing rises up from the

The Lesser Heavenly Circulation

虛六流周不動變

靈六流周居不動變

abdomen, and they meet in this area. Movement is used to circulate this breath (oxygen) inside the body. It goes to many parts of the body and becomes energy.

The *shen* (spirit/vitality) should be concentrated inside, making the practitioner more calm, without being exposed externally. Lao-tzu wrote: "One with the great wisdom appears like a fool. . . . There should be brightness without shine." In this principle, T'ai Chi Ch'uan differs from other exercises.

Keep all of the movements smooth and round, neither convex nor concave.

The movement of the T'ai Chi Ch'uan should be compared to the invisible machine. The movements should be like wheels, flowing without hindrance and working efficiently.

The inner energy is rooted in the feet, and flows upward through the legs. It is directed by the waist and expressed by the fingers. The movements of the feet, legs and waist should be integrated; they should move as a unit. In this way, the practitioner can advance and retreat freely and can gain advantage in any movement.

This passage compares the body to a tree. First, energy comes from the feet, the roots; then it travels up the leg, which is like the base of the tree, to the waist, which is like the trunk of the tree. This is the most important part of the tree, because it stands on the ground and resists any attack from storms outside. Inside, nutrition is brought from the ground to nourish the branches. The branches always carry out the functions, producing the leaves, flowers, and fruit, but actually they are controlled and supported by the trunk. Thus you can gain advantage both in time and position.

If your position is disadvantageous, your movements will be confused and broken. You should correct the problem in your legs and waist.

This passage refers to the importance of the legs and the waist. The legs transmit the energy from the feet, which are like the root; the waist directs and controls the energy, like an axis. If the legs and waist are balanced and correct, you will feel comfortable and relaxed. If the position of the legs and waist is incorrect, it will be uncomfortable both physically and mentally, and your form will be less efficient. If your position is unbalanced, look for the problem in your leg or waist.

The movements of upward, downward, forward and backward all come from the legs and the waist. All the movements are controlled by the mind, not by the outside.

Each movement must have an opposite. The upward must have a downward; a left should have a right, and a forward should have a backward. This movement is inside, not outside.

This is the principle that comes from the Chinese philosophy, *I Ching,* the *yin* and the *yang,* Heaven and Earth, day and night. These opposites complement each other.

In self-defense you can respond to any attack like a snake. If the head is attacked, it can respond with the tail, and if the tail is attacked, the head can respond. If it is attacked in the middle, it can respond with both head and tail. If it is attacked in both the head and the tail, it can respond with the middle of the body.

When we practice the form there should be a balance of left and right. For instance, in Single Whip, the left hand has the power of the attack; at the same instant, the right hand balances. Likewise, in Slant Flying, the right hand attacks while the left hand balances the body. When there is an upward movement there must, at the same instant, be a balanced downward movement. In Crane Spreads Wings, as the right hand moves up, protecting the forehead, the left hand sinks down with a little power, balancing the form. In Grasp Bird's Tail, as the left hand moves up the right sinks down, simultaneously balancing the form. In Wave Hands Like Clouds and in Step Back and Repulse Monkey, both hands alternate from heavy to light, without the light being absolutely empty, so the movement remains balanced.

In addition to this balance within each form, there is also balance within the forms as a whole and between forms. In practicing the individual forms, the practitioner can follow Brush Knee and Push, a forward move, with Step Back and Repulse Monkey, a backward move. The Single Whip (high), can be combined with Snake Creeps Down (low), followed by its opposite, Golden Cock Stands on One Leg (high). There is a left and right Kick with Toes, and a left and right Hit Tiger. Left and right movements alternate in Wave Hands Like Clouds. When there is a left, there should be a right; when there is an up, there should be a down.

Before moving upward, one must first move downward. This means lifting something upward and then destroying it downward. If the root of the object is lifted, it can be destroyed easily.

In self-defense the practitioner must first shake his opponent's balance, causing his foot to move from the ground. Then he can push him easily. This is called *t'i fang. T'i* means "lift up"; *fang* means "push" (releasing energy, like shooting an arrow).

Solid and empty must be differentiated. Every part of the body has a solid and an empty aspect. In addition, the body as a whole has a solid and an empty aspect. The unity of the body must be maintained, linking all of the parts together without any separation.

This passage means that the practitioner must make one leg heavy and the other light. In some forms, one leg has 70 percent of the weight, the other 30 percent. When changing to a new form or moving in a new direction, the solid leg bears 100 percent of the weight; the moving leg should be entirely light. This applies not only to the legs, but also to the arms—for example, in Slant Flying the right hand is heavy and the left hand is light.

The whole body should be united so that it can move effectively for health and self-defense, just as the parts of a machine must be united. If the parts of a machine are too tight or too loose, it cannot work effectively. A change of even one millimeter can make it more efficient. Similarly, if one place is too loose in the body—in the large joints (neck, shoulders, elbows, hips, knees, wrists, ankles) or in the small joints (between the phalanges of the fingers and between the vertebrae of the spine)—the body cannot move freely and efficiently.

In sum, the movements must be coordinated and balanced, like a machine or like a tree. The body and mind must be coordinated too, moving in a united and harmonious way, without serial disconnection, which detracts from the efficiency of the form. If the machine is disconnected, it becomes inefficient or useless. In the same manner, if the tree branch is disconnected from the trunk, the branch will wither. If the body is disconnected from the *chi,* the body will eventually sicken and grow weak.

The Relation Between the Thirteen Postures and Eight Trigrams, The Five Elements in the T'ai Chi Tu

The movement of the "Long Exercise" [T'ai Chi Ch'uan] is like a long river and a great sea, flowing unceasingly.

The Long Exercise refers to T'ai Chi Ch'uan (originally there were 108 movements), in which the movements are very gentle and continuous, like a long river. There is no rushing, no separation, but it is very powerful; also like a great sea it is peaceful on the surface but deep and powerful below. Even though it appears soft, like water, it is very strong.

In the *Tao Te Ching,* Chapter 8, it is written:

> The highest goodness, water-like,
> Does good to everything and goes
> Unmurmuring to places men despise,
> But so, is close in nature to the way (tao).

Water can ascend to heaven (clouds) or descend into the earth (springs); it can wash away dirt, nourish the withered, just as in T'ai Chi Ch'uan, the *chi* and the blood circulate down to the feet and up to the crown of the head, and in this movement they wash away poisons and nourish the tissues.

The first eight movements are symbolized in the Pa Kua, the eight trigrams. The postures are: "Push Up" (Ward Off), "Pull Back" (Roll Back), "Press Forward" (Chi), "Push Forward" (Ah), "Pull Down" (Tsai), "Bend Backward" (Lieh), "Elbow Stroke" (Chou), and "Shoulder Stroke" (Kao) (see the following figure).

These eight trigrams correspond to the T'ai Chi Tu or Great Primal Beginning, which comes from the *I Ching*. In the *Ta Chuan* it says:

Therefore there is in the Changes the Great Primal Beginning. This generates the two primary forces. The two primary forces generate the four images. The four images generate the eight trigrams.

The first four movements—Push Up, Pull Back, Press Forward, and Push Forward—represent the four directions: south, north, west and east. (See *T'ai Chi Ch'uan and I Ching,* 2nd edition, Second Series, for further explanation of these postures.)

The second four postures represent the four corners: southeast, northeast, southwest, and northwest. The form Sea Bottom Needle is an example of Pull Down *(Tsai).* Bend Backward *(Lieh)* is similar to Slant Flying and Wild Horse Ruffling Its Mane (in the long form). Elbow Stroke *(Chou)* is contained in the *Ta Lu;* also the elbow is extended following a shoulder strike. Shoulder Strike *(Kao)* is contained in the form Step Forward and Strike with Shoulder.

There are five steps: Advance *(Chin),* Retreat *(Tuei),* Step and Look to the Left *(Ku),* Step and Look to the Right *(P'an);* and Stand Firm in the Middle *(Chung ting).*

These five steps correspond to the five elements. They are: metal, wood, fire, water, and earth. This theory of the five elements comes from the diagram of Chou Tun-yi of the Sung dynasty. His commentaries explain the way in which the diagram symbolizes the production and evolution of all things.

The empty circle at the top represents the Supreme Ultimate *(T'ai Chi),* which produces the *yang* through movement and the *yin* through quiescence. The circle below it, with its concentric inner

The Great Primal Beginning

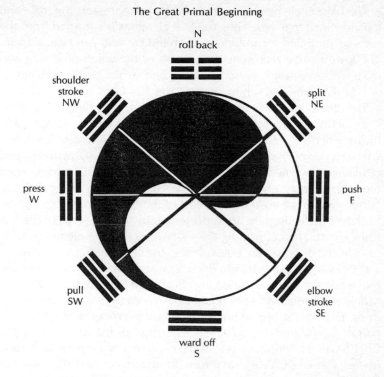

circles of alternating black and white, represents the opposition and interaction between *yin* and *yang*. It can be seen that the *yang* side contains *yin* within it and the *yin* side contains *yang* within it. Below this circle there is a pattern that contains five smaller circles. They represent the five elements, which come into being through the interaction between *yin* and *yang*. As Chou Tun-yi's commentary explains it:

By the transformations of the *yang,* and the union therewith of the *yin,* water, fire, wood, metal, and earth are produced. These five elements become diffused in harmonious order, and the four seasons proceed in their course.

The Five Elements are the one *yin* and *yang;* the *yin* and *yang* are the one Supreme Ultimate; and the Supreme Ultimate is fundamentally the Ultimateless. The Five Elements come into being each having its own particular nature. [Feng Yu-lan, *History of Chinese Philosophy*]

The large circle below the five small ones represents the male and female joined together. Thus the five elements are formed from the *yin* and *yang* and recombine to form the *yin* and *yang* once again. The lowest circle represents the results of the union of female and male (*yin* and *yang*): the production and evolution of all things.

This diagram is closely related to the T'ai Chi Ch'uan.

The uppermost circle represents emptiness. In the beginning of the T'ai Chi Ch'uan, the player stands quietly and his mind is empty. The movements of T'ai Chi Ch'uan correspond to the alternate black and white stripes of the second circle of the diagram. Downward and retreating movements represent the *yin,* and upward and forward movements represent the *yang.* The eight trigrams of the *I Ching* correspond to the eight movements of the hands. The five elements as shown in the diagram are represented by the five steps of the T'ai Chi Ch'uan. The connecting lines between the five elements, both straight and diagonal, are equivalent to the constant movement of the T'ai Chi Ch'uan. The straight lines represent forward and backward movements as in Brush Knee and Push and Step Back and Repulse Monkey. The diagonal lines relate to diagonal steps as in Slant Flying, Bring Tiger to the Mountain, and Fair Lady Works at Shuttles. This part of the diagram is equivalent to a chart of the footwork of T'ai Chi Ch'uan. The bottom circle of the diagram corresponds to the end of the T'ai Chi Ch'uan—a return to stillness *(Wu Ch'i)* (see the following diagram).

This classic of T'ai Chi Ch'uan was written by the great master, Chang San-feng, founder of T'ai Chi Ch'uan. Defense was a secondary function. The art was chiefly to prolong life and preserve youth. This is the primary purpose of T'ai Chi Ch'uan, as was noted by Master Yang Lu-ch'an (1799–1872).

Recently, during the T'ai Chi Ch'uan National Convention, in Wuhan City, China, Master Wu Tu-nan performed T'ai Chi. Although one hundred years old he performed the movements in a relaxed, flowing manner without the slightest appearance of old age. When I read Master Wu's book, in the 1920s, in Shanghai, I recall reading how his grandfather had wondered how this young man (Master Wu) could perform great and heroic deeds for his nation, because his body was so weak. Today it is more than obvious that Master Wu practiced T'ai Chi for health and longevity. His

The T'ai Chi T'u of Chou Tun-yi*

DIAGRAM OF THE SUPREME ULTIMATE

The Ultimateless!
Yet also the Supreme Ultimate!

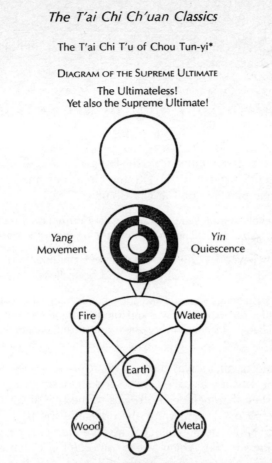

Yang
Movement

Yin
Quiescence

Fire

Water

Earth

Wood

Metal

The Ch'ien Principle
becomes the male
element

The K'un Principle
becomes the female
element

Production and Evolution of
All Things

*Feng Yu-lan, op. cit., p. 436.

picture appeared in the magazine *China Sports* and also in many American magazines.

T'ai Chi Ch'uan Ching, by Wong Tsung Yueh

This treatise is continued from the last part of *T'ai Chi Ch'uan Lun,* which discusses the T'ai Chi T'u (the Great Beginning). This is the fundamental principle of T'ai Chi Ch'uan.

T'ai Chi is evolved from Wu Chi (the Negative Terminus). It is the source of movement *(yang)* and stillness *(yin)* and the mother of *yin* and *yang.*

It was believed by the ancient Chinese philosophers that at the beginning the universe was empty and boundless.

There was something undefined and complete, coming into existence before Heaven and Earth. How still it was and formless, standing alone, and undergoing no change, reaching everywhere and in no danger [of being exhausted]. [*The Texts of Taoism.* James Legge, trans. p. 67, 25.1.]

This state of affairs was termed *Wu Chi.* From this state arose movement, which was called *yang,* and stillness, which was called *yin.* The state that includes both was termed "T'ai Chi."

The theory of *yin* and *yang* then became the basis of Chinese philosophy and Natural Science. The Five Elements (五行) and the Eight Trigrams (八卦), which are so important in Chinese literature, owe their origin to the theory of *yin* and *yang.* Also from this theory was developed the principle of body fitness and the fundamental principle of Chinese medical science.

All great thinkers have known there is a harmonious relationship in all things. This harmony comes from two opposites that complement each other in the order of nature. The world is composed of these opposites. For example, there is Heaven and Earth, night and day, male and female. The Chinese employ *yin* and *yang* as two terms for these two opposing attributes.

Let me introduce the historical background of the T'ai Chi T'u, which originated in prehistoric times. Even in very ancient times the people used a round symbol with a light upper half, representing heaven, and dark lower half, representing earth. The whole symbol is said to have represented man, who is a union of both light and dark components. There may be some truth in this tradition, but it is not supported by clear historical or archaeological evidence. In any case, the oldest written expression of the principle underlying these diagrams is in the *I Ching,* in Chapter 11 of Ta Ch'uan (see the *T'ai Chi Ch'uan Lun,* p. 10). The *I Ching* itself contains no T'ai Chi T'u diagram, but the relevance of this quoted passage for the diagrams will become clear in the explanation that follows.

According to some authorities on Chinese cultural history, including Richard Wilhelm,[6] the term *t'ai chi* originally referred to the ridgepole of a house, the horizontal beam at the very top of the roof where the two slanted parts of the roof meet. This topmost pole of the house divides the roof into two parts which face in opposite directions. Because of the direction from which the sun shines on the house, one side of the roof is brighter, representing *yang,* and the other side is darker, representing *yin.* Of course, this is constantly in flux as the day progresses and the sun moves across the sky. The side that faces the rising sun and is thus strongly *yang* in the morning gradually becomes less bright, and the other side, strongly *yin* in the morning, becomes brighter, until the relationship is completely reversed in the evening. Only at a single moment, perhaps at high noon, are the two sides of the roof equally bright. Thus the roof of the house divided by its ridgepole can be regarded as a symbol of the eternal cycle of alternation that continuously goes on between the two fundamental forces of *yin* and *yang.* It may have been that this symbol was sufficient in prehistoric times, and that special written diagrams were only invented much later.

By the time of the Sung dynasty (A.D. 960–1279) complex diagrams were developed, and extensive commentaries were written that explained their meaning. Of particular importance were the diagram and commentary entitled *T'ai Chi T'u—Shuo* (Diagram of the Supreme Ultimate Explained), composed by the philosopher Chou Tun-yi (1017–73).

Master Wang Chung-yueh's writing is more easily illustrated by using Chou Tun-yi's T'ai Chi T'u diagram of the Supreme Ultimate. At the top, the white circle is empty. The inside is called *Wu Chi,* the second one, containing black and white stripes, is the T'ai Chi.

The black is *yin,* the white is *yang.* When they move, they separate and go down to the square basket that contains five small circles. This represents five elements: water, wood, fire, metal, and earth.

Between the small circles there are a straight line and a diagonal line, which show their relationship. They grow and conquer each other until at last, complementing each other, they combine and become quiet. Then they go down to the next white circle and become *Wu Chi* (stillness) again.

T'ai Chi Ch'uan is based on the T'ai Chi symbol. This symbol contains the *yin* and the *yang,* which are the substantial and insubstantial, the firm and the yielding. The movements are circular and flow continuously, always changing, and when done correctly also have beauty and skill, and become an art.

The principle of continuous change comes from the philosophy of Confucius; *chuang,* which means center. The T'ai Chi Ch'uan form should be in equilibrium. The body should be in perfect balance without inclining to either side. Both outside and inside should be peaceful and quiet, in perfect harmony. In daily practice and in self-defense; the practitioner should wait for an advantageous position to deal with his opponent and use the attitude to respond to the opponent's attack. There is more detail on this subject the introduction to this book.

When it is moving it opens and when it is still it closes.

This means there are two opposing movements, which correspond to the T'ai Chi symbol and the movement of the T'ai Chi Ch'uan.

The T'ai Chi Ch'uan form should be neither done in excess nor insufficiently. When your opponent is open and stretched, you should yield and curve; you might expand when your opponent is curved.

The first sentence refers to the practice of forms in a middle area, neither overdoing nor underdoing them. The second sentence refers to push-hands and self-defense, where one must yield to the opponent's strength but not separate from the opponent's movement. This meaning continues in the next passage.

When the opponent uses strength against me and I yield, it is called "withdrawing." When the opponent is at a disadvantage, it is favorable for me.

Then I move toward him, not allowing him to retreat. This is called "to adhere."

The principle of T'ai Chi Ch'uan is yielding before force. When force is employed, the practitioner moves away or changes direction. Adhering is the reverse. When the opponent retreats, follow closely. This action is like a person's shadow. It cannot be pushed away, it cannot be separated. Some people call T'ai Chi Ch'uan "shadow boxing."

This action is not only applied as a method of personal self-defense but is also used by the Chinese Army as a method of military strategy when training their guerrillas. "When the enemy is advancing, I retreat, and when he retreats, I follow him closely, not letting him escape. When he stops, I disturb him, not letting him rest." Using this method the guerrillas defeated the Nationalist Army and won the wars of Korea and Vietnam, fighting against the Americans.

Respond quickly to the opponent's fast action and slowly to his slow action. Even through thousands of changes of movement, the principle is the same.

This means that when the opponent attacks quickly, I answer with a quick movement. When he attacks slowly, I respond with a slow movement. Even though there are many techniques, this principle prevails.

From familiarity and practice you come to know your opponent's intentions. With this understanding gradually comes spiritual enlightenment. This stage cannot be reached without long effort.

To achieve spiritual enlightenment, one must learn the correct method of doing the exercises, then practice push-hands to understand the opponent's intentions. Through many years of effort you will reach the stage of spiritual enlightenment.

The energy ascends to the top of the head lightly. The *chi* of vitality sinks down to the *tan tien*.

This passage has only two short sentences, but it is very important to the practice of T'ai Chi Ch'uan. This is to join the *Tu Mu* and the *Jen Mu*, which means the Greater Heavenly Circulation.

Thus the practitioner should straighten the spine and relax the neck, letting the vital energy reach the crown of the head. The second sentence refers to the *chi* of vitality sinking down to the *tan tien*. This important place should be described clearly; many books refer to one and a half, one and a third, or three inches below the navel, among the intestines. *Tan tien* means the Sea of Breathing. According to human anatomy, this place is a bit like a small bag. If the *chi* is sinking down to it, it is more active. If it is without *chi,* it is empty and cannot be a bag. In Taoist terminology it is a stove, where water can be boiled and becomes steam, where the elements of the five inner organs can be purified to become the *ching,* sperm, and the *ching* can be refined to be the *chi.* In scientific terms, the breath *(chi)* sinks down to this place. The mind mobilizes the nerves, which apply energy (like electricity), making the area hot so that it performs the function of a stove, evaporating the water to steam. This reduces sickness and increases energy, thus promoting health and longevity.

Keep the body straight without inclining to either side. [Spiritual vitality] is suddenly hidden and suddenly appears.

The body should be perfectly balanced, without inclining to either side, in complete equilibrium. Both the mind and body should be relaxed, the spirit and the *chi* of vitality can function without the opponent's knowledge.

When there is an attack to the left, it is responded to by yielding on the left side. The right side yields when the attack is to the right.

This means use the yielding in response to strength. Then you can neutralize the opponent's power and continue with a counterattack. Practitioners who use strength against strength run the risk of injuring each other.

When the opponent attacks high, I seem higher, and when he attacks low, I appear lower. When he advances I yield and seem further away, and when he retreats I follow him and I seem closer.

If the T'ai Chi Ch'uan master practices for a long time, his body becomes more resilient, his ligaments longer, and his joints looser. His body can sometimes be stretched like a cat's; then the opponent cannot touch him. When the opponent wants to push him up, he can stretch his body and become higher. When the opponent wants to press him down, his body yields, lower than the pressure of his opponent. When the opponent wants to advance, the practioner can use the resilience of his legs and waist and retreat much farther than he can be reached. When he wants to retreat, the practitioner can stretch his body and extend his leg like elastic, and follow the opponent close to his body, so he cannot get away. When the opponent loses his balance, the practitioner can push him away. If the practitioner's body can stretch one or two inches further than the opponent's, he should win.

A feather cannot touch his body nor a fly alight on it.

The T'ai Chi master has developed a sensibility like radar and an unconscious response to the lightest force acting on his body. For example, if someone attacked a master of the *yang* family secretly, from behind, the attacker fell back as if he had been touched by electricity.

The opponents don't know my intentions, but I know theirs. The T'ai Chi master is without competition.

Through long practice, both mental and physical ability are increased. The T'ai Chi master can hide his own motives, but he can detect the opponent's intention. He can always defeat his opponents. Thus, the *I Ching* says:

The superior man knows what is hidden and what is evident. He knows weakness. He knows strength as well. Hence the myriads look up to him.

There are many kinds of martial arts, but even when techniques are different, generally the stronger always wins over the weaker, and the quicker over the slower. These are inherent qualities not attained by study.

This passage refers to many kinds of martial arts that merely use strength and quickness—contrary to T'ai Chi Ch'uan, which uses yielding and borrowing the opponent's strength against him and is more skillful. This follows Lao-tzu's idea:

The softest thing in the world dashes against and overcomes the hardest. That which has no [substantial] existence enters where there is no crevice. [*The Texts of Taoism,* Part I, p. 87.]

A few ounces can move a thousand pounds. This shows that strength isn't necessary to prevail over strength. The winner of the battle is not always the strong.

This means a trigger force can move a very heavy object. A few ounces of trigger power can move a thousand-pound object, just as the steering wheel can control and change the direction of a car.

Some older men can defend themselves when they are attacked by many people. Obviously this does not depend on speed.

There are many stories in China about the old T'ai Chi Ch'uan master with a humble manner, who declines a challenge, but when he cannot avoid fighting uses his spiritual vitality and subdues his opponents.

Stand balanced as a scale or move as actively as a wheel.

One should stand perfectly balanced, like a scale, not inclined to either side. When one moves, one should be agile, like a circling wheel.

If the weight sinks to one side it can be moved, or yields easily. If the weight is on both sides, there will be stagnation.

The T'ai Chi Ch'uan practitioner should put his weight on one foot. When the moving foot is absolutely light, he can move nimbly. If he puts weight on both feet, there is stagnation, and the entire body cannot move. If the weight is put on one side, it is called "single weightedness"; if it is put on both sides, it is called "double weightedness."

There are many people who have studied T'ai Chi Ch'uan for years who don't understand this principle. They cannot neutralize the opponent's force and are easily defeated by others. This is because they are using double weight.

The T'ai Chi Ch'uan practitioner should be perfectly balanced so that he can move nimbly. When this principle is applied to self-defense, he can neutralize the opponent's attacking force and continue with a counterattack. Otherwise, he will be subdued by his opponents.

To avoid this weakness, one must understand the principle of *yin* and *yang*. "Sticking" is also "Moving Away," and "Moving Away" is also "Sticking." *Yin* cannot leave the *yang,* and *yang* cannot leave the *yin. Yin* and *yang* complement each other, and this is the basis of understanding force.

If you want to avoid the mistake of double weightedness, you must understand the principle of *yin-yang,* or substantial and insubstantial. When the opponent attacks your left side, you must be yielding and shift your weight to the rear leg to neutralize the opponent's attacking force. By turning your body to the left, you can counterattack with your right hand, which becomes *yang.* The *yin* and *yang* cannot be separated but should complement each other. This is called interpreting force.

After one has learned to understand force and practices diligently to develop one's ability and achieves a high degree of the arts, with silent contemplation one can reach the stage where one's actions absolutely follow the mind.

If the T'ai Chi Ch'uan player practices the forms and the Push Hands for a long time, gradually he can reach the highest points, his action merely cooperating with his mind. He can understand the opponent's attacking force and deal with him easily. Finally, if the practitioner masters the arts of T'ai Chi Ch'uan, he can reach spiritual enlightenment.

The fundamental principle of T'ai Chi Ch'uan is to forget oneself and follow the opponent. Many people misunderstand this and ignore the near to seek the far. If you make a mistake of one inch in the beginning, you will miss your target by a thousand miles.

In other words, one should forget oneself. Applying this principle to self-defense: When the opponent pushes forward, his intention goes forward; if you respond with pulling back, you can easily throw him. If the opponent pulls you, you can counter with Push Forward or Shoulder Strike, because his intention is to move backward. If you insist on your own idea, you will be using strength against strength. Even if you defeat your opponent, you will waste energy and run the risk of injury.

Many people want to achieve results quickly or to reach the high points without laying a foundation. In my experience, many students don't practice the form correctly, but they want to learn Push Hands and then Ta Lu; they want to study many theories, but they do not understand the practical application. In the end, they achieve nothing. The student should be very careful in the beginning; then he can progress without mistakes. As the last sentence of the passage says, a mistake of one millimeter in the beginning can cause an error of a thousand miles at the end.

The Principle of the Thirteen Postures

This part of the Treatise was written by Wu Yu-hsiang, a T'ai Chi Ch'uan master of the Ch'ing Dynasty, although it is credited by some to Wang Chung-yueh, a Ming Dynasty master. Whoever the author is, the ideas are very important to the teaching of T'ai Chi Ch'uan.

The word *chi* has several aspects. One is the outer aspect, in which it refers to the atmosphere and the breath. Another aspect is inside the body, where *chi* refers to oxygen or vitality. Chuang-tzu, the second great Taoist master (c. 300 B.C.), said that the common man breathes with his throat while the real man breathes with his heels. What he means is that the real man recognizes that proper breathing entails bringing the fresh air into the body, circulating oxygen throughout the body and expelling the waste gases such as carbon dioxide.

In the Chin Dynasty (A.D. 300) an enlightened Taoist master and medical doctor, Ko Hung, said that man is in the air and air is in the man. He recognized the different aspects of the *chi*. The Taoist and T'ai Chi Ch'uan master can purify and refine the *chi* to become inner energy, or vitality. In Taoist terminology the *ching* (sperm), the *chi* (vitality), and the *shen* (spirit) are always mutually produced within a cycle. It is like the cycle of rainfall, in which water is first evaporated from the earth, the water vapor forms clouds, and the proper conditions produce rainfall. For more details of the process, see my *T'ai Chi Ch'uan and Meditation,* Chapter 4: "The Tao of Breathing."

Use the mind, concentrated, calm and quiet, to direct the *chi,* letting it sink down to the abdomen. It can penetrate to the bones.

This passage is similar to the theory of Mencius, the second great sage of Confucian ideas. In his writings he says that the mind is the commander of the *chi*. So apparently he is not referring to the common breathing, where no effort of mind is involved. The T'ai Chi Ch'uan uses movement and the mind combined with the breathing and is very efficient. First the *chi* sinks down to the abdomen, where it combines with the blood and other elements of the five inner organs. In the presence of the heat within the body it follows the blood circulation and penetrates the bones to become marrow.

Many people think the bone is impermeable, but when the blood and other elements combine with the *chi* in the presence of the heat of the body, they become like steam and can penetrate the bones. Of course, it only penetrates a small measure each time, so it is most beneficial to practice the exercise each day. If we examine the joints, we see that there are many tendons and sinews connected to the bones, where the *chi* can penetrate the bones. Furthermore, if we examine a dry bone we will discover many small holes. The bones of young people are solid and heavy because there is an abundance of marrow, making the bones resilient. When people grow old the bone marrow is exhausted and the bones become light and brittle and can be easily broken. Thus the marrow in the bones is capable of increasing and decreasing, although the process is invisible.

T'ai Chi Ch'uan is an exercise to be performed daily. When done accurately and continuously, it can increase the vitality. It is an especially good exercise for the middle-aged and even more important for older people. The Taoist call it replenishing the oil in the lantern to make it burn longer and brighter.

Use the *chi* to move the body smoothly and it can easily follow your will.

When the *chi* becomes the inner energy, it is similar to the gas or steam that propels a modern piece of machinery. If the machine is running smoothly and effectively, it will perform its functions according to the direction of the operator, just as the body will be propelled by the *chi* according to the directions of the mind. A good car, if it is a well-oiled machine, will allow the driver to go fast, carry a heavy load, turn left or right, all according to his will.

I discovered that not only can one use the *chi* to move the body, but also the movements of T'ai Chi Ch'uan can guide the *chi* inside the body, which can make the *chi* and blood circulation move easily. For details, see Chapter 6, ''Taoist Meditation and T'ai Chi Ch'uan,'' and also my book *T'ai Chi Ch'uan and Meditation* (Schocken), Chapter 6, "Special Movements of T'ai Chi Ch'uan for Meditation," with illustrations of each movement guiding the *chi* to a different area.

With the body erect you feel as if your head is suspended by a thread hanging from above; it is called Ting Tan Ch'uan. You can feel your spirit lift up and then your movements are light and supple without feeling heavy or clumsy.

When your spinal cord is erect, every vertebra connects with the next, like beads on a string. Physically your energy can come from the leg through the coccyx and up the spinal cord to the crown of the head. The joints of the body move freely like a puppet on a string. Psychologically, with the neck erect your spirit of vitality can rise with the physical energy to the *ni-wan,* Gate of Heaven.

The mind and the breath *(chi)* interchange automatically. This makes the movements supple and rounded. This is solidity changing to emptiness.

The coordination of the breath and the movement is important to T'ai Chi Ch'uan. Then you can feel your movement is more natural and resilient, both physically and psychologically. When you practice the form, you bring fresh air into the body and expel the toxic air. In self-defense, this can help you to be more agile and to avoid internal injury.

Manifestation of the energy should be quiet, relaxed, and concentrated, with your aim on one point.

This passage refers to self-defense. You should concentrate your mind and physical energy to attack one point, just as when you shoot an arrow, you must concentrate both your mind and your strength in order to hit the target. You should employ this idea whenever you practice the form, not only for self defense. In each movement you should be thinking what its purpose is for self-defense, until it becomes a natural process. When you are really fighting, you should be relaxed, not tense. It will make your mind and body free. As the T'ai Chi master says: "When you practice your form it should be as if you are really fighting. When you are fighting, your mind should be free, as if you are playing with children.

Stand comfortably straight and centered, then you can deal with the eight directions.

This means balance: Both for the daily practice of the forms and for self-defense you should be standing straight and centered like a ramrod. This is very important for balance when practicing the forms. It makes your body feel more comfortable and responsive and also protects you from injury. For self-defense, whether you attack or are attacked, if you have your center of gravity it is easy to deal with attacks from any direction.

This passage is the core of T'ai Chi Ch'uan. It is also an important idea in the philosophy of the *I Ching.* The Chinese words *chung* and *cheng* are found in many places in the *Book of Changes. Chung* is "the middle and the center." *Cheng* is "correct, straight." Together these words refer to being both correct and with perfect balance.

Let the *chi* penetrate to every part of the body, into the cells and the bones.

When your body is completely relaxed and the mind is concentrated, the *chi* can reach everywhere. Even the fingertips, skin, and bones. This is important for health. The *chi* can propel the blood to go to every part of the body. It washes the dirty places, reduces poisons, and nourishes the skin. You can avoid many sicknesses, both internal and external, especially the tumor which represents a stagnation of the blood. The *chi* makes your body warm and the skin moist and fresh, becoming like a plant receiving water and fertilizer that will have flowers that are fresh and colorful.

Employ energy like hundred-times refined steel,
Nothing can resist it.

This passage refers to self-defense in which you concentrate your mind and employ your energy.

The attitude should be like a falcon, ready to attack the rabbit; the mind [spirit] is concentrated like a cat ready to pounce on a mouse.

This passage refers to Push Hands and self-defense. The falcon circling above the rabbit is calmly looking for a chance to attack. Like a cat waiting to pounce, it is alert. In Push Hands there are many continuous movements until a chance comes, and suddenly one can attack.

Still like a mountain; active like a river.

This passage refers to the manner of the T'ai Chi practitioner. When he is quiet like a mountain, he is firm outside and quiet inside. When he is moving he is like a river whose water is flowing gently, but whose power is very strong. Nothing can resist it. It can penetrate the mountain and break the dam.

We can compare the T'ai Chi Ch'uan movement to a river. If the the water flows too fast, it will damage the banks; if it runs too slowly, sand will accumulate, which could cause flooding. The T'ai Chi Ch'uan movement should be flowing and gentle; otherwise it can cause many kinds of injury or sickness. The water of the river is good for irrigation and navigation; the T'ai Chi Ch'uan movements can improve blood circulation, nourish the body, and clean the poison or dirt out of the tissues.

Accumulate energy like drawing a bow; release energy like shooting the arrow.

"When one wishes to expand, one must first contract. When one wishes to be strong, one must first be weak" (*Tao Teh Ching,* Chapter 36).

The form is curved but employs a straight line. The energy should always be stored, ready to be used at any time for attack.

This describes the form of T'ai Chi Ch'uan. The arms, legs, even fingers are always curved. Only the spinal cord is always straight. The energy always moves inside in a straight line, just as the arrow moves straight from the curved bow. The energy always hides inside, not appearing outside. Therefore T'ai Chi Ch'uan is called the esoteric school.

Power is released from the spinal cord; when the steps change, they follow the movement of the trunk of the body.

The movements of T'ai Chi Ch'uan are completely coordinated. The movements of the limbs follow the movements of the trunk, and the whole body moves as a single unit.

To hold back is to attack; to attack is to hold back. If the energy is separated, it is immediately rejoined.

The movements of hold back and attack are in interaction. For example, when an opponent attacks the left side of your body, you neutralize his attacking energy by withdrawing and turning your body to the left. Simultaneously you attack him with your right hand.

To and fro movements should be one continuous folding action. Advance and retreat should alternate.

The movement of the two hands should be folding and turning from left to right. For self-defense purposes, this can be applied for sticking and neutralizing, push and pull. The step should be forward and backward for the purpose of attacking and neutralizing.

If one is extremely soft and flexible, one can become extremely strong and solid.

The T'ai Chi Ch'uan practitioner should try to make his body soft and flexible. The result, over a long time, is that the body can become extremely strong and solid. For example, the air (ether) is very soft, but a hurricane or whirlwind can destroy many buildings or carry a boat into the air. Also, if air is compressed into a tire, the tire becomes hard as a rock and can bear many tons for a long distance.

If one exhales and inhales correctly, the body is agile and alert.

T'ai Chi Ch'uan movements should be coordinated with the breathing. Thus, when you advance, inhale, when you retreat exhale; when the movement is up, inhale; when it is down, exhale; when the movement is open, inhale; when it is closed, exhale. If breathing is done correctly, it makes the movements more agile. It helps physically to make the movements smoother and mentally more peaceful. This technique can be applied to self-defense, for T'ai Chi Ch'uan and for meditation. If you practice correctly and unceasingly, you can achieve health, longevity, even immortality.

The *chi* should be cultivated harmoniously and carefully.

The term *chi* refers not only to air and breathing but also to intrinsic energy. My friend, Dr. William Chao, a Chinese medical doctor who introduced the term "life energy," wrote a book called *Principle of Life Energy.* Recently, many books have used this term. It means the energy for life. The Taoists emphasized *chi* as one of the three treasures of the body. Therefore, it is important for T'ai Chi

Ch'uan and meditation. If we develop and refine it purposefully, without being disturbed by the six sentiments (anger, love, hate, fear, desire, happiness), we can attain health, longevity, and self-defense.

The *chi,* or intrinsic energy, should be stored curved so that the energy is inexhaustible.

This idea is exactly what Chuang-tzu referred to in his book (p. 298): "Not subjecting your body to toil, not agitating your vital force —then you may live for long."

The mind is like the commander; the *chi* is like the flag, and the waist is like the pole of the banner.

The terms "commander," "flag," and "banner" were used in Chinese military action in ancient times. It represents the mind commanding the *chi,* the *chi* mobilizing the body.

The form of the movements in the beginning should be open and expanded; later, they should be reduced in size.

At the beginning one practices with large circular movements; this gives relaxation and a feeling of comfort. Gradually, one reduces the size of the movements as the skill increases. When you begin practicing the T'ai Chi Ch'uan forms, your posture should be open and stretched, which will relax your muscles and loosen your joints. Your blood will circulate freely; thus, your body becomes stronger. Your mind becomes peaceful. Gradually your posture should be reduced in size. Make the cycle of movement slower and slower, until it is invisible. Then you can become proficient.

When the opponent is still, I am still also. If he makes the slightest movement, I will move and reach him first.

This continues the idea in the last passage; when the cycle is invisible, you can move more quickly than your opponent and reach him first even if he moved before you. This principle is used in Push Hand and can be applied to self-defense. Therefore you should pay full attention to your daily practice. When you deal with opponents, you should be relaxed, both mentally and physically, as if you were playing with children. Then, you can defeat your opponents easily.

When the T'ai Chi Ch'uan Master is dealing with an opponent, his manner is quiet, like a cat waiting to pounce on the mouse. When he senses the opponent's readiness to move, he can move and attack him first. This ability should be developed by practicing Push Hands.

The *ching,* or energy, seems to be relaxed but really isn't. The form seems open, but it is not quite open. Even when the energy seems broken, your attention still continues.

The *ching* seems relaxed but not overrelaxed; if it is too relaxed, it will be broken. The form seems open, but it is not wide open; if it was overexpanded, it would seem to be broken and you could not reach the highest point. Sometimes the energy seems disconnected but the intention still continues.

The mind is primary, the movement of the body is secondary; as, if the abdomen is completely relaxed, the *chi* or vitality can penetrate to the bones. The mind remains at ease and the body is quiet.

This idea should be kept in mind at all times. This passage refers to mind as more important than movement of the body. As we have seen, when the abdomen is completely relaxed, the *chi* sinks down into the *tan tien* and penetrates to the bones.

You must remember: the body must move as a unit. When one part moves, another part follows; when one part is still all parts are still.

You must remember that when you act, every part should move, and when you are still, all parts should be tranquil. This passage describes the movement of the whole body, which should be coordinated at all times, like the parts of a machine. Then it can work efficiently.

By the movement of your arms to and fro, guide the *chi* to the back, and collect the energy into the spinal cord.

When you move your arms to and fro—as in Push Up, Pull Back, and Press Forward—energy is produced. The mind is used to guide the chi of vitality to the back and collect it into the spinal cord.

Show quietness on the outside. This could develop the spirit of vitality inside, and show quiescence and harmony outside.

This continues the idea from the last passage. When the energy is stored in the spinal cord, it can strengthen the spirit of vitality because the spinal cord is part of the central nervous system.

T'ai Chi Ch'uan footwork must be quiet and sure like a cat. It must be very even and slow, like reeling silk from a cocoon.

This passage describes the movement of T'ai Chi Ch'uan—the steps should be as light and firm as a cat walking. The mobilized *chi* of energy should be gentle, slow, continuous, and even, not too quick and not intermittent. By diligently practicing these concepts, you will achieve mental and bodily harmony and reach the highest form of enlightenment.

The whole body and mind are entirely guided by the spirit. Do not overemphasize the *chi* of vitality; if you do so, the *chi* of vitality will grow slow and stagnate. When you reach the *chi* of vitality, the muscle strength is diminished. When your *chi* is diminished, your body becomes like a purified spirit.

This passage is a bit confusing. Actually, there are three stages. Most people use muscle strength. When one reaches a certain level in T'ai Chi Ch'uan, one uses less muscle strength. When one reaches the highest points, the *chi* of vitality becomes refined to spiritual vitality. Thus, the highest points, like meditation, transfer the *ching* (sperm) to *chi* of vitality. The second stage transforms the *chi* of vitality to *shen,* spiritual vitality. When meditation reaches the last stage, one can stop breathing and stop the pulse; this is called the Great Quiescence.

For self-defense, as if the *chi* of vitality has disappeared, the body becomes as solid as refined steel. For example, when Joe Louis, the king of boxing, visited Taiwan on December 13, 1951, a seventy-year-old Chinese master, Kuo Jian-ru, challenged him to strike him with three punches without counterattack. Joe Louis declined—if he defeated the man, it would be no surprise, but if he did not, his reputation would decline. Mr. Kuo also demonstrated many wonderful techniques. He held a long knife by the blade in his hand, tied it with string, and let people try to pull it out of his hand by the handle. His hand was not harmed. Also he let people slash his face with a sharp knife, but his face was not harmed. His hands and his face were like steel. (This story appeared in *Ch'un Chiu* magazine, August 1, 1984, p. 15).

Another story refers to Master Tu Shing-wu. Many people know him as a legendary figure of the martial arts in China. Once he let his student Jiang Kuo-Chang strike him with full strength. He flew away by Master Tu Shing-wu's reflected invisible power and sat on a table twenty steps away. Many people in the audience did not know why he flew away. The student thought he had been careless and wanted to try again. The next time, the student concentrated all his attention, but again he flew away and sat in the same place on the table. (This story also appeared in *Ch'un Chiu,* March 16, 1986, pp. 22–24.)

Scientifically speaking, the *chi* can be compared to steam or gas. The spirit may be like electricity. With a little touch, there can be great movement or great hurt. Thus Master Tu's energy became spiritual and he reached the stage of electricity.

The *chi* is compared to the wheel and the waist is compared to the axis of the wheel.

The *chi* moves within the body actively. The *chi* is round in shape like a wheel. In action it moves like a wheel, either left to right, as in Wave Hands Like Clouds, or from front to back, as in Step Back and Repulse Monkey, or around the back, as in Fair Lady Works at Shuttles. The waist should be straight, upright, like the axis of the wheel.

Do not neglect any of the thirteen postures.
The source of the will and the life energy is in the waist.
Pay attention to the change from substantial to insubstantial.
Then the Chi will flow through the whole body without interruption.

The Song of the Thirteen Postures

This stanza asserts the importance of the thirteen postures with particular attention to the waist, because the will and the life energy are in the region of the kidneys, which are within the waist. If you do the form carefully, paying attention to the changes from heavy to light, the *chi* will flow through your whole body.

Motion develops from stillness; motion and stillness are similar.
You can get wonderful results when the changes in motion and stillness
  follow your opponent's motive.
Pay attention to every movement, and
You can achieve effortless skill.

This paragraph asserts that motion and stillness develop each other. If you achieve this, you can overcome your opponents easily.

You should at all times pay attention to the waist.
With abdomen relaxed and light, the *chi* can be activated in the whole body.
If the coccyx is erect and centralized, the *shen* (Spirit of Vitality) will rise to the top of the head.
The body will feel agile and flexible
When the head is held as if suspended from a string.

The waist is an important part of T'ai Chi Ch'uan. Full attention should be paid to it at all times. It is like an axis; the abdomen is in the front, where the *chi* of Vitality develops. If it is relaxed, the *chi* will pervade the whole body. The coccyx and the spine are important in the back, where the nerve centers are located. If the back is erect and relaxed, the *shen* (Spirit of Vitality) will rise up to the top of your head. Your body will feel light and nimble, as if your head were suspended by a string.

> Be careful to study the principle of T'ai Chi Ch'uan.
> Bent and extended, open and closed
> Follow the natural course.
> In the beginning, you should be guided orally by a teacher.
> Gradually, as one studies unceasingly
> Skill will increase.

This stanza states that the movements of bending and stretching, opening and closing are important elements of every movement of T'ai Chi Ch'uan. If you move naturally, you can achieve the technique. This technique is guided by a teacher in the beginning; later success is 90 percent dependent on practice alone.

> If you ask, what is the principle of T'ai Chi Ch'uan,
> The mind is the master and the body the subordinate.
> What is the aim of T'ai Chi Ch'uan?
> Health and longevity and rejuvenation
> Keep the body in an eternal spring.

This is the important philosophy of T'ai Chi Ch'uan, that the mind should direct the body like a commander and that the body should follow the direction of the mind. The purpose of the T'ai Chi Ch'uan is good health and longevity, keeping the body eternally lively, warm, and relaxed, like springtime, not with a body like dry wood and a mind like cold ashes.

> Each word of this song is important.
> If you do not follow the idea of this song,
>   you will waste your time and regret your loss.

NOTES

The *I Ching* passages in this book are quoted from *The I Ching: Or Book of Changes,* translated by Richard Wilhelm, rendered into English by Cary F. Baynes (Third Edition; Princeton: Princeton University Press, 1950, © 1967) and are cited by book and page number.

I. INTRODUCTION

1. Book II, pp. 348–349.

IV. THE FORMS AND THE HEXAGRAMS

1. Book III, p. 560; Book I, p. 137.
2. Book I, p. 8; Book I, p. 9; Book I, p. 9.
3. Book II, p. 280.
4. Book III, p. 636.
5. Book III, p. 474.
6. Book I, p. 134; Book I, p. 134.
7. Book I, p. 76.
8. Book I, p. 142; Book I, p. 140.
9. Book III, p. 653; Book I, pp. 201–202.
10. Book I, p. 110.
11. Book I, p. 130; Book III, p. 551.
12. Book I, p. 112.
13. Book I, p. 105.
14. Book I, p. 113; Book I, p. 114; Book I, p. 242.
15. Book I, p. 165.
16. Book I, p. 23.
17. Book I, p. 89.
18. Book I, p. 101.
19. Book I, p. 17.
20. Book I, p. 33; Book I, p. 34; Book I, p. 34.

21. Book I, p. 198.
22. Book I, p. 66; Book III, p. 465.
23. Book III, p. 695.
24. Book I, p. 213; Book I, p. 214; Book II, p. 277; Book III, p. 670.
25. Book I, p. 251.
26. Book III, p. 585.

V. T'AI CHI CH'UAN USED FOR SELF-DEFENSE

1. Book II, p. 316.

There's an epidemic with 27 million victims. And no visible symptoms.

It's an epidemic of people who can't read.

Believe it or not, 27 million Americans are functionally illiterate, about one adult in five.

The solution to this problem is you... when you join the fight against illiteracy. So call the Coalition for Literacy at toll-free **1-800-228-8813** and volunteer.

**Volunteer
Against Illiteracy.
The only degree you need
is a degree of caring.**

Ad Council Coalition for Literacy